"Steven Christie has given manual for speaking with one of the most complicated and emotional issues. This book will help us in our care and defense of the most vulnerable, as we seek to build a culture that cherishes the holiness and beauty of human life and a society where it is easier for people to love and to raise families."

MOST REVEREND JOSÉ H. GOMEZ,
Archbishop of Los Angeles

"I warmly recommend *Speaking for the Unborn* to anyone who is involved in the Pro-Life fight. In a concise, persuasive, and rational way, it counters all of the standard Pro-Choice arguments. It will prove enormously helpful in addressing the most pressing moral issue of our time."

BISHOP ROBERT BARRON,
Founder, Word on Fire

"'The truth will set you free,' Jesus tells us, and Steven Christie uses the truth to outline simple, cogent responses to the arguments advanced by Pro-Choice advocates. This manual provides short, honest, and irrefutable Pro-Life talking points, presented in an easy-to-grasp style, all designed to win hearts and minds to the Pro-Life position."

TIMOTHY CARDINAL DOLAN,
Archbishop of New York

"I cannot think of an author better prepared to write an omnibus of answers to Pro-Choice arguments. Steven Christie holds advanced degrees in medicine and law—and he knows the arguments well, since he once advanced them himself. This book should be a textbook in mandatory courses on reality. It's a must-read."

SCOTT HAHN,
Founder, St. Paul Center for Biblical Theology
and Author of Hope to Die

"No class of human beings should ever be denied the legal protection of the law, and yet this is precisely what permissive abortion laws do. Drawing on both his medical and legal expertise, Steven Christie has produced the handbook you need to defend the rights of the unborn. Speaking for the Unborn will equip you to speak up for those who can't."

RYAN T. ANDERSON,
President, Ethics and Public Policy Center

"Abortion continues in America because of euphemisms. This book is a great light—a practical resource for being part of the solution. Be not afraid to talk about abortion in a culture drowning in the darkness of the culture of death. Help women choose life and talk about the great possibilities of life. Dr. Christie, with this book, and in his life, helps us make progress."

KATHRYN JEAN LOPEZ,
Senior Fellow, National Review Institute
and Editor-at-Large, National Review

"Abortion is one of the gravest abominations that affect mankind. In *Speaking for the Unborn*, Dr. Steven Christie offers very clear, convincing, and often witty answers to almost every possible argument in favor of abortion. This is a great resource to have, and the beautiful photos of the children in the womb speak for themselves."

FR. JUAN R. VÉLEZ,
Former M.D. and Author of
Passion for Truth: The Life of John Henry Newman

"The Pro-Life movement has needed an up-to-date handbook of brief but effective replies to the slogans and arguments in support of legal abortion. Do the cause of truth a favor and share this book with as many young persons as you can."

MICHAEL PAKALUK,
Professor of Ethics and Social Philosophy,
The Catholic University of America

"With his background as a physician, attorney, and father of five, Dr. Christie provides intelligent and compassionate rebuttals to the common pro-choice arguments. Whether debating abortion in the U.S. Capitol or discussing the issue over the backyard fence, *Speaking for the Unborn* is an invaluable resource for anyone defending the right to life for unborn children."

DANIEL LIPINSKI,
Member of Congress, 2005–2021

Speaking
for the
Unborn

Speaking
for the
Unborn

30-Second Pro-Life Rebuttals
to Pro-Choice Arguments

Steven A. Christie, M.D., J.D.

EMMAUS
ROAD
PUBLISHING

Steubenville, Ohio
www.emmausroad.org

Emmaus Road Publishing

1468 Parkview Circle

Steubenville, Ohio 43952

Library of Congress Control Number: 2021948752

ISBN: 978-1-64585-187-5 (paperback)

978-1-64585-188-2 (ebook)

Cover design by Desry Turnip

Layout by Emily Demary & Allison Merrick

For my wife, Grazie, and our children—
Nicholas, Grazie, Lucas, William, and Luli—
without whom I would be completely lost.

Acknowledgments

The bulk of the arguments and rebuttals included here are not original with me. They incorporate the work of many Pro-Life leaders and thinkers. Source materials include books, journals, Pro-Life websites, speech transcripts, and online video presentations. In fact, in many parts of this book, I am more *editor* than author.

I have tried to present the strongest and most persuasive rebuttals possible. In doing so—or trying to do so—I have incorporated the direct and modified quotes of others' work. I want to specifically acknowledge my reliance on the extraordinary work of Randy Alcorn, Scott Klusendorf, Brian Fisher, Trent Horn, Greg Koukl, Bob Schwarzwalder, Lila Rose, Francis Beckwith, Christopher Kaczor, Carter Snead, Ben Shapiro, and Ramesh Ponnuru.

I also want to thank my wife and the many friends who have offered helpful criticism and suggestions during the writing of this book, especially Fernando Perez and Mark Mulholland.

I also owe a great debt to Fr. Jay Alvarez for his direction in matters both spiritual and practical, without which I would have missed out on so much of the goodness in my life.

As the last thing I want to do here is take credit for work that is not mine, each argument and rebuttal presented includes its source materials. However, since there is so much overlap and redundancy in the manner in which many authors present these arguments, I kindly ask that you notify me if you believe I've not given proper credit, so I can immediately make the appropriate corrections.

Lastly, I would like to give special thanks to David Reinhard for his wise counsel, patience, and hard work in the professional editing of this manuscript.

TABLE OF CONTENTS

FOREWORD

"THE TRUTH WILL OUT."—William Shakespeare

A couple of years ago, I was at a Pro-Life rally holding a sign that said *"Adoption is a Loving Option"* when a car abruptly pulled to a stop next to me.

A woman rolled down her window and yelled at me, "What makes you think you know a damned thing about abortion?!"

I wanted to respond, but she immediately sped off, dismissing me with an obscene gesture.

If I'd had the chance, I would have told her:

- As a physician, I'm well versed in the science of embryology.
- As a lawyer, I've studied the law and the Constitution.
- As a father of five, I know a bit about pregnancy and babies.
- As a husband of twenty-five years, I've come to understand the challenges women face in the struggle to balance the demands of career and family life.

- And as a family man, I know that men are at their best when they exercise deep loyalties to women and children.

And while all these facts are true, my most important credential is the fact that I spent the first thirty-five years of my life as a secular Pro-Choice liberal.

So I know exactly what, why, and how the other side thinks about abortion.

And having lived in both the Pro-Choice and Pro-Life worlds, I have a fairly unique vantage point from which to analyze the abortion debate.

When I was Pro-Choice, I learned the arguments.

When I became Pro-Life, though, I learned the truth.

And the truth was what I so desperately wanted to tell that angry woman who yelled at me and then sped away.

And because I could not tell her, I now tell you.

The truth will out.

COMPANION VIDEO TUTORIAL

Ideally, this book is intended to be utilized *after* watching its **companion video tutorial**—a one-stop shop for everything you should know about abortion in order to be an effective Pro-Life advocate.

This four-part, sixty-minute video covers the following:

- What is abortion?
- Constitutional law cases
- Current state of affairs
- Science and embryology
- Key definitions
- Abortion procedures (explanations and animations)
- Planned Parenthood
- Pro-Life strategies
- What you can do

You can watch this video tutorial at **www.SpeakingForTheUnborn.org**.

Once you have viewed the important background material contained in this video, you will be ready to start learning and effectively using the Pro-Life rebuttals contained in this book.

I have worked very hard to make these rebuttals clear, practical, user-friendly, concise, and—most importantly—effective.

So give the video a look and let's get to work!

Thanks!

Steve

PS: Your feedback is very important to me. If you have criticisms or suggestions, please let me know via email at **Steve@SpeakingForTheUnborn.org**.

"Abortion degrades and damages everyone it touches: the baby, the mother and the doctor."

—ANONYMOUS

WHY BOTHER?

Since Roe v. Wade in 1973, there have been more than sixty-two million abortions performed in the United States.[1]

If the unborn are not alive or not human, then it really doesn't matter, and we needn't bother about this.

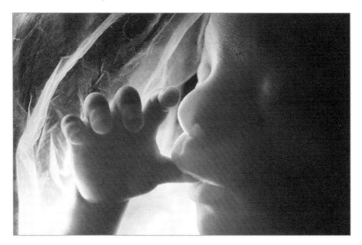

If, however, the unborn *are* alive and *are* human, then we have killed more than sixty-two million children.[1]

Children.
That's why we bother.
It's that simple.

1   David Sivak, "Fact Check: Have There Been 60 Million Abortions Since Roe v. Wade?" Check Your Fact, July 3, 2018, https://checkyourfact.com/2018/07/03/fact-check-60-million-abortions/.

"The fight for the right to life is not the cause of a special few, but the cause of every man, woman, and child who cares not only about his or her own family, but the whole family of man."

—MILDRED JEFFERSON

STRATEGY

The Pro-Life movement relies on basic facts, science, and truth to spread its message.

The Pro-Choice movement, on the other hand, survives by denying the truth of abortion—employing rhetorical deception, trite clichés and ad hominem attacks, branding their opponents as morons, misogynists, or both.

Inevitably, their arguments boil down to a single falsehood: "Sex is *liberating* and should be without consequences."

Of course, preserving this falsehood takes great effort. Why? Because the "consequences" of "liberating" sex are nothing less than the broken bodies of unborn children and a culture of death that degrades women, children, and families.

And denying the truth of abortion is hard work. It requires a concerted effort to be *blind* to the truth, to be *deaf* to the truth, and to never ever *speak* the truth.

Our job, then, is to reveal the truth to those who desperately do not wish to see it, hear it, or speak it. And to do so with intelligence, diligence, and—perhaps most importantly—compassion.

But we cannot accomplish our task by simply winning *arguments*. We must focus on winning *hearts*.

And winning hearts takes patience, kindness, perseverance, and a mastery of the facts surrounding abortion.

In the end, our constant goal is to hear these words at the end of every discussion or debate: "You know, that's interesting. I'd never really thought about it that way before. . . ." That is the sound of a heart opening to the truth.

HOW WE SPEAK

Our success in opening hearts to the truth depends on not only the words we say, but how we say them. The following comprise a strategy for approaching these conversations:

- We speak charitably, intelligently, and persuasively—relying only on facts.

- We make clear, simple arguments (no complex philosophical "proofs").
- We are brief (no rebuttal longer than thirty seconds).
- We are always mindful that nearly 25% of the women we will speak with have already had an abortion. Many of these women suffer deeply, and they deserve our compassion.

WHAT WE SPEAK

- A fully memorized, but naturally delivered, thirty-second summary of "Why I Am Pro-Life" (a sample summary is included in this book)
- The Pro-Life arguments
- The rebuttals to the Pro-Choice arguments
- The truth (no tricks, no gimmicks, and no "gotchas")

NO RELIGIOUS ARGUMENTS

The vast majority of abortion advocates are secular liberals who think religious people are unsophisticated, unthinking, brainwashed, backward, and intolerant Jesus-freaks.

So if you happen to be religious and are debating a non-religious person about abortion and you've made ten very compelling, non-religious arguments for protecting the unborn, but then you happen to mention "God" or "sanctity of life" or "sin" or "Bible" . . .

Well, you'll suddenly see the face of the person you're speaking with dramatically change. You can then immediately read their mind, which is saying something like this: *Ohhhh, ohhhh, ohhhh. I'm sorry. I hadn't realized you were a freak. Have a nice day.* And then every rational, non-religious argument you made just vanishes.

I've come to learn that making a religious argument is simply handing your opponent a huge club with which to beat you over the head.

We have many, many compelling non-religious arguments that powerfully explain why abortion is wrong. Let's stick to them.[2]

FIGHTIN' WORDS

There is much debate among those in the Pro-Life movement as to how we should refer to (1) the unborn, (2) the act of abortion, and (3) those who support a right to abortion.

---

2   Author's Note: If you are Catholic, or just curious, you can read about the Catholic Church's formal position on abortion at the end of this book.

As to the **unborn**, I generally use the term "unborn child." It is simple, accurate, and honest. It is also advantageous that Merriam-Webster defines "child" as an "unborn or recently born person."[3]

As to the **act of abortion**, I keep it simple as well. An abortion is the *intentional ending of an innocent life*, and "killing" (as per Merriam-Webster) is to *"cause the death of."*[4] Therefore, I refer to abortion as "the intentional killing of an unborn child."

While the term "killing" is entirely accurate, some may prefer to say "ending the life of an unborn child" or "the destruction of a living human being." Gauge your audience and use what feels right.

Pro-Choice advocates obviously hate terms like "child" or "killing," but I don't believe we should let them reframe this debate inaccurately by using disingenuous and deceptive phrases, such as "products of conception," "non-viable clump of cells," or "ending a pregnancy."

As to how to refer to **those who support a right to abortion**, I personally use the term "Pro-Choice"

---

3   *Merriam-Webster's Collegiate Dictionary*, s.v. "child," accessed August 14, 2021, https://www.merriam-webster.com/dictionary/child.
4   *Merriam-Webster's Collegiate Dictionary*, s.v. "killing," accessed August 14, 2021, https://www.merriam-webster.com/dictionary/killing.

rather than "Pro-Abortion." I do so for several reasons. One, I find it fosters more productive debate. Two, many supporters of abortion rights still find the act abhorrent. Three, I ask others to refer to me with the label that I prefer—"Pro-Life" instead of "Anti-Woman" or "Anti-Choice"—and it seems only fair to reciprocate.

If you are uncomfortable with any of my preferred terms, please replace them with those that work best for you. But remember, the point is winning the hearts and minds of others, and not necessarily giving vent to the words that feel good or righteous to you.

COURAGE

It takes courage to speak up against abortion in today's modern secular culture—a culture that so fiercely advocates for "sex without consequences."

Whenever and wherever you speak up, you will be ridiculed and maligned, and will be called "extremist," "misogynist," "intolerant," "moron," and worse.

But the fear of ridicule must not deter you.

And when you do find yourself lacking in courage, remind yourself that in this great cause of defending the unborn, there is really only one thing to fear: remaining silent.

"WHY I AM PRO-LIFE" IN THIRTY SECONDS

This manual includes my thirty-second summary of "Why I Am Pro-Life." It is critical that you prepare your own version (or use mine) and have it fully memorized.

My experience is that the opportunity to defend the Pro-Life position is pretty common and often arises unexpectedly. You may only get one chance to make your case. So make it count.

If you can make an articulate, respectful, and persuasive argument in only thirty seconds, you have a real chance to win hearts and minds. If you are unprepared, however, you may waste what might be your only opportunity to make an effective case for life.

So prepare your thirty-second summary. Practice it over and over again. See that it becomes a part of you. Then, be ready to use it at a moment's notice!

REBUTTALS

Each Pro-Choice argument is followed by a rebuttal or a set of possible rebuttals. Beneath each rebuttal are its sources and citations.

Articulating our Pro-Life positions does not require strict memorization of each rebuttal. In fact, canned counterarguments can turn off your audience and may not reflect the nuance or particulars of the argument at hand. That said, being intimately familiar with each specific argument is critical if you are to be successful.

Agile and effective refutation will require you to practice (*and practice*) these rebuttals over and over again. I've found that repeating a rebuttal aloud at least five times within a two-week period usually does the trick.

Ideally, practice these rebuttals with a debate partner. Begin by reading them aloud to each other. Say the words exactly as though you were trying to convince someone you really care about and respect. Those you are trying to persuade need to know you care—care about them and care about others—before they come to care about what you know.

After a few practice rounds of reading from the page, repeat the argument without looking at the words.

Practice, practice, practice!

Of course, no single rebuttal in this manual will likely convert anyone. They will be effective, however, if they are *cleverly pieced together* over a five- to ten-minute conversation.

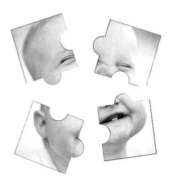 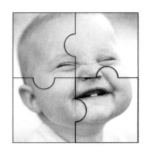

The goal is to form a coherent picture of the truth.

These rebuttals, while relying on the work of many well-known experts in the field, reflect my own personal style of thinking and speaking. My style, however, might not be your style.

If you're uncomfortable with my language or strategic approaches, modify them to meet your needs and the needs of your audience. Please, make this manual your own.

A Few Basic Definitions

Embryo: The unborn from the end of Week 1 through Week 8

Fetus: The unborn from the end of Week 8 until birth

Human Being: A member of the species Homo sapiens

Life/Alive/Living: Whether something is "alive" is a purely scientific question that science has fully settled. To be "alive," the following criteria must be met:

- Cellular organization
- Growth and development
- Metabolism (ability to capture, make, or utilize energy)
- Homeostasis (ability to maintain an internal equilibrium)
- Responsive to stimuli
- Reproductive capacity
- Contains all the genetic information needed to control its development for its lifetime[5]

---

5   Dominic Corsini, "8 Characteristics of Life in Biology," Study.com, accessed October 11, 2021, https://study.com/academy/lesson/8-characteristics-of-life-in-biology.html.

All seven of these criteria for life are met at conception.[6] This is a biological fact attested to by the American College of Pediatricians and nearly every embryology textbook used in medical schools.[7] Even Planned Parenthood has admitted that life begins at conception, stating in one of their very own publications that "abortion kills life after it has begun."[8]

Person: Defining "person" does not require complex philosophical or metaphysical analysis, despite claims to the contrary. Its definition is clear and simple, and found in nearly every dictionary. As Merriam-Webster states, *as its very first definition,* a "person" is a "human."[9]

Body Part: Science defines "body part" as a structure that shares the same genetic code as the rest of the body (e.g., appendix, arm, tonsils, or heart) and does not direct its own development.[10]

6   M. L. Condic, comp., "The Origin of Human Life at Fertilization: Quotes from Medical Textbooks and Peer-Reviewed Scientific Literature," Bioethics Defense Fund, updated September 2017, https://bdfund.org/wp-content/uploads/2016/05/Condic-Sources-Embryology.pdf-old.

7   "When Human Life Begins," American College of Pediatricians, March 2017, https://acpeds.org/position-statements/when-human-life-begins.

8   Birth Control Federation of America (Planned Parenthood), *Plan Your Family for Health and Happiness,* copy available in the Sophia Smith Collection at Smith College in Northampton, MA, accessed August 14, 2021, https://libex.smith.edu/omeka/items/show/440.

9   *Merriam-Webster's Collegiate Dictionary,* s.v. "person," accessed August 14, 2021, https://www.merriam-webster.com/dictionary/person.

10   Randy Alcorn, "Is the Unborn Part of the Mother's Body?" Eternal Perspective Ministries, March 29, 2010, https://www.epm.org/resources/2010/Mar/29/unborn-part-mothers-body/.

BASIC DEVELOPMENTAL MILESTONES:

- Day 1:   A fully alive human being, with unique DNA
- Week 5: Heart beating
- Week 6: Brain activity is present
- Week 9: Baby sighs, stretches, moves head, opens mouth, sucks thumb
- Week 13: Body sensitive to touch
- Week 21: Potentially viable[11]

---

11   Jacqueline Howard, "Born before 22 Weeks, 'Most Premature' Baby Is Now Thriving," CNN, November 11, 2017, https://www.cnn.com/2017/11/08/health/premature-baby-21-weeks-survivor-profile/index.html.

"Why I Am Pro-Life" (in Thirty Seconds)

I am Pro-Life:

- **Because I am Pro-Science**: There is overwhelming scientific consensus that life begins at conception.

- **Because Social Justice Begins in the Womb**: Every living human being is entitled to the most fundamental of human rights: the right to "life" itself. Because being a burden on someone is never justification for killing them.

- **Because I am Pro-Woman**: Abortion degrades women, treating their fertility as a defect, enabling men to use and then abandon women when they are most vulnerable. Abortion never empowers women—only the men who wish to exploit them.

- **Because I am Against Violence**: Abortion is not only immoral, but is an act of extreme violence against the most innocent and vulnerable.

- **Because of the Visible Evidence**: Ultrasound and MRI now clearly reveal to the world what's moving inside a woman's body: *a living baby.*

- **Because of Objective Morality**: If abortion is the killing of an innocent unborn child, then it's immoral and cowardly to remain silent.

That's why I am Pro-Life.

So why do you think abortion is OK?

- "When Human Life Begins," American College of Pediatricians.

- *The American Heritage Medical Dictionary*, reprint (2008), s.v. "life."

- Keith L. Moore, T. V. N. Persaud, and Mark G. Torchia, *The Developing Human: Clinically Oriented Embryology*, 10th ed. (Philadelphia: Saunders, 2016), 11.

- Gary C. Schoenwolf et al., *Larsen's Human Embryology*, 5th ed. (Philadelphia: Churchill Livingstone, 2015), 2, 14.

- Bryan Kemper, *Social Justice Begins in the Womb* (Magnolia TX: Lucid Books, 2009).

- Ben Shapiro, "March for Life Speech" (Washington, DC, January 17, 2019).

- Carter Snead, "A Bioethical Argument against Abortion," EWTN Pro-Life Weekly, March 18, 2017, YouTube video, 3:42, https://www.youtube.com/watch?v=hbM0hHkwJq0.

- Landrum Brewer Shettles and David M. Rorvik, *Rites of Life: The Scientific Evidence for Life before Birth* (Grand Rapids: Zondervan, 1983), 112–13.

CATEGORY 1:

IT'S NOT "ALIVE" OR "HUMAN" OR A "PERSON"

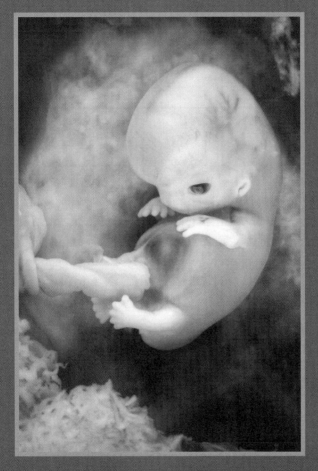

(WEEK 8)

A FETUS OR EMBRYO IS NOT ALIVE.

IT'S JUST A CLUMP OF CELLS.

NOBODY REALLY KNOWS WHEN LIFE BEGINS. IT'S REALLY

A PERSONAL OR PHILOSOPHICAL OR RELIGIOUS QUESTION.

FIRST REBUTTAL

Whether or not something is "alive" is a not a matter of philosophy or religion or politics. It's a purely scientific question that science has fully settled. There's over-whelming scientific consensus that, from the moment of conception, an embryo fulfills all seven criteria of biological life—as stated by the American College of Pediatricians and nearly every medical school text-book. So what you're trying to call a mere "clump of cells" is, by definition, a living human being.

- "When Human Life Begins," American College of Pediatricians.
- The American Heritage Medical Dictionary, s.v. "life."
- Moore, Persaud, and Torchia, The Developing Human, 11.
- Schoenwolf et al., Larsen's Human Embryology, 2, 14.
- Christopher Kaczor, The Ethics of Abortion: Women's Rights, Human Life, and the Question of Justice, 2nd ed. (Abingdon, UK: Routledge, 2015), 70, 112.
- Randy Alcorn, ProLife Answers to ProChoice Arguments, 3rd ed. (Colorado Springs: Multnomah, 2000), 51.

- Steve Jacobs, "I Asked Thousands of Biologists When Life Begins. The Answer Wasn't Popular," Quillette, October 16, 2019, https://quillette. com/2019/10/16/i-asked-thousands-of-biologists-when-life-begins-the-answer-wasnt-popular/.

SECOND REBUTTAL

Look. Life begins at conception—and that's a simple scientific fact that is no longer even debated in the scientific community. The largest recent survey of over 5,000 biologists from 1,000 worldwide institutions revealed that a full 96% agreed with the statement "Human life begins at conception." And they were not a collection of Pro-Life, religious, or conservative scientists. In fact, these biologists self-described as 89% "liberal," 85% "pro-choice," and 63% "non-religious." So let's please stick to the most basic scientific fact in this debate: life begins at conception.

- Jacobs, "I Asked Thousands of Biologists When Life Begins."

THIRD REBUTTAL

If you want to talk about when human life actually begins, there's really not much to discuss. The science is fully settled on this. Overwhelming scientific consensus holds that life begins at conception. What the Pro-Choice movement is really talking about is not "when something is alive" but "when you think a baby's life begins to matter." And that's not a scientific question at all. Pro-Choicers are simply deciding which human lives they deem *undeserving of life.*

- Shapiro, "March for Life Speech."
- "When Human Life Begins," American College of Pediatricians.
- *The American Heritage Medical Dictionary,* s.v. "life."
- Moore, Persaud, and Torchia, *The Developing Human,* 11.
- Schoenwolf et al., *Larsen's Human Embryology,* 2, 14.
- Kaczor, *The Ethics of Abortion,* 70, 112.
- Alcorn, *ProLife Answers,* 51.
- Jacobs, "I Asked Thousands of Biologists When Life Begins."

FOURTH REBUTTAL

Even the former Director of Planned Parenthood, Dr. Alan Guttmacher, wrote that "when fertilization has taken place, a baby has been conceived."

- Shettles and Rorvik, *Rites of Life,* 112–13.

FIFTH REBUTTAL

Even Planned Parenthood, the United States' largest abortion provider, admits that life begins at conception. It said in its own publication that "abortion kills life after it has begun."

- Birth Control Federation of America (Planned Parenthood), *Plan Your Family for Health and Happiness.*

SIXTH REBUTTAL

If we define "death" as the "cessation of a heartbeat and

brainwaves," why shouldn't the "*existence* of a heartbeat and brainwaves" define "life"?

- Alcorn, ProLife Answers, 67.
- Trent Horn, *Persuasive Pro-Life: How to Talk about Our Culture's Toughest Issue* (El Cajon, CA: Catholic Answers, 2014), 139–40.

SEVENTH REBUTTAL

Here's a question to consider: What would the headline of every newspaper around the world be if just a single, tiny, solitary living cell was found on the surface of Mars?

- Lila Rose, "On Mars, a single cell would be considered LIFE," Facebook, December 7, 2018, https://www.facebook.com/lilagracerose/photos/ on-mars-a-single-cell-would-be-considered-life-however- on-earth-a-human-being-in/10157034074073000/.
- Shapiro, "March for Life Speech."

Worldviews

'A Fetus Is Just A Clump Of Cells,' Says Slightly Older, Larger Clump Of Cells

June 4th, 2021 – BabylonBee.com

9.3k Shares · 7.2k SHARE · 965 SHARE · ✉ SHARE

CEDAR HILLS, OR—While discussing the hot-button issue of abortion with a friend over coffee on Friday, local woman Cindy Carson claimed a fetus is just a clump of cells, despite herself being just a slightly older, larger, more organized clump of cells.

Pro-Choice Argument #3

OK, SO MAYBE AN EMBRYO IS TECHNICALLY "ALIVE."
BUT SO IS AN ACORN OR A TOMATO OR A JELLYFISH—AND
WE DON'T WORRY ABOUT THEIR LIVES. DO YOU ALSO
FRET OVER KILLING A LIVING JELLYFISH?

REBUTTAL

A jellyfish (or an acorn or a tomato) is a thing. An embryo or fetus is a human being. And all human beings, unlike "things," have inherent dignity and immense intrinsic value, irrespective of their capacities. Surely you are not arguing that all living things have equal intrinsic value—that there would be no difference between killing, for example, a two-year-old cow and killing a two-year-old child? Clearly, that is not the case. We simply do not kill innocent human beings.

- Alcorn, ProLife Answers, 71–73.

- Horn, Persuasive Pro-Life, 129–35.

- Jay Watts, "Acorns and Embryos," Merely Human Ministries, August 28, 2019, https://merelyhumanministries.org/acorns-and-embryos/.

Pro-Choice Arguments #4 and #5

A FETUS OR EMBRYO IS NOT A HUMAN BEING.
IT'S JUST A "POTENTIAL" HUMAN BEING.

AN EMBRYO IS NO MORE HUMAN THAN AN ACORN IS AN
OAK TREE. A FETUS MIGHT EVENTUALLY BECOME A
HUMAN, JUST AS AN ACORN MIGHT EVENTUALLY BECOME
A TREE, BUT AN EMBRYO IS NOT YET A HUMAN BEING.

FIRST REBUTTAL

There's simply no such thing as a "potential human."
It's an unscientific, made-up term. Being human is not
a matter of degrees. You're either human or you're not.
To be human is to be a member of the species Homo
sapiens. Nothing more. Nothing less. The unborn are
fully living, genetically unique members of our species.
Science makes this perfectly clear. They might be
smaller, weaker, and less developed, but they're living
human beings.

- Francis J. Beckwith, Taking Rites Seriously: Law, Politics, and the Reasonableness of Faith (New York: Cambridge University Press, 2015), 119.

- Alcorn, ProLife Answers, 71–72.

- Horn, Persuasive Pro-Life, 120–22.

SECOND REBUTTAL

When a woman has an "embryo" or "fetus" inside her, she is not carrying a "non-human". Embryo and fetus are simply two stages in the *development* of living humans—no different than the terms "toddler" or "adolescent." An embryo doesn't *become* a human being; an embryo is a human being.

- Alcorn, ProLife Answers, 63.
- Scott Klusendorf, "Stepping up to Defend Life," Focus on the Family, February 25, 2019, YouTube video, 27:53, https://www.youtube.com/watch?v=kg0_G-3xTvk.
- Horn, Persuasive Pro-Life, 129–35.
- Kaczor, The Ethics of Abortion, 14–15.

Life

Joyful Pro-Choice Mother Throws Fetus Shower

December 23rd, 2016 · Babylonbee.com

SAN LUIS OBISPO, CA—Expectant mother Erin Bruford was described as "glowing" as the five-months-pregnant woman enjoyed the company of her friends and family at her fetus shower this Thursday evening, thrown to celebrate the parasitic growth within her womb.

Pro-Choice Argument #6

A FETUS OR EMBRYO IS NOT A "PERSON"—AND ONLY
PERSONS HAVE RIGHTS IN THE CONSTITUTION.

FIRST REBUTTAL

"Personhood" is a manufactured term. It serves no
purpose other than to exclude, marginalize, or subju-
gate a class of "undesirable" people. History is littered
with examples of how "personhood" has been used as a
weapon to dehumanize and deny the most basic rights
of life and liberty to "undesirables"—blacks, women,
Jews, immigrants . . . the list goes on. It's now time
for the unborn to also escape this victimization. Social
justice begins in the womb.

- Akhil Rajasekar, "Why It Doesn't Matter If the
  Unborn Aren't Persons," The Federalist, January
  10, 2019, https://thefederalist.com/2019/01/10/
  doesnt-matter-unborn-arent-persons/.

- Kaczor, The Ethics of Abortion, 128.

- Alcorn, ProLife Answers, 82.

- Kemper, Social Justice Begins in the Womb.

SECOND REBUTTAL

A civilized society doesn't assign "personhood" on the
basis of size or capability—unless you're ready to call

the disabled, the frail, or those in comas "non-persons" and undeserving of life. Humanity, not size or ability, imparts personhood. The only thing required to be a "person" is to be a member of our species.

- Kaczor, The Ethics of Abortion, 30, 41, 59, 100.
- Jonathan Leeman and Matthew Arbo, "Why Abortion Makes Sense," The Gospel Coalition, June 1, 2016, https://www.thegospelcoalition.org/article/why-abortion-makes-sense/.
- Alcorn, ProLife Answers, 74, 75, 82, 105.
- Brian Fisher, "Here's How to Stop Any Pro-Choice Argument in Its Tracks," Human Coalition, May 27, 2014, https://www.humancoalition.org/2014/05/27/huco-helps-unravel-thorny-pro-abortion-arguments/.

THIRD REBUTTAL

When it comes to "personhood," let's not pretend we're dealing with some complex philosophical question of metaphysics. The definition of "person" is simple and straightforward. Merriam-Webster, for example, says, as its very first definition, that a "person" is a "human." Pretty simple.

- Merriam-Webster's Collegiate Dictionary, s.v. "person."

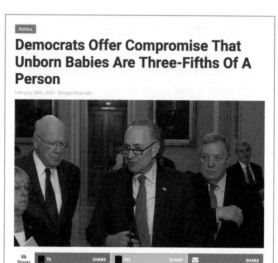

Politics

Democrats Offer Compromise That Unborn Babies Are Three-Fifths Of A Person

February 28th, 2021 · BabylonBee.com

WASHINGTON, D.C.—In a historic compromise, Democrats in Congress have conceded to allow limited constitutional protections for unborn babies as three-fifths of a person.

Pro-Choice Argument #7

AN EMBRYO OR FETUS IS JUST PART OF A WOMAN'S BODY,
AND A WOMAN CAN DO WHATEVER SHE WANTS
WITH HER OWN BODY.

REBUTTAL

The embryo is—in no way—a "part" of the mother's body. Science clearly defines "body part" as a structure that shares the same genetic code as the rest of the body (like the appendix, arm, tonsils, or heart) and does not direct its own development. The unborn child has a completely unique genetic code. Half of the time it even has a different sex! It also directs its own development. So the embryo is clearly a *separate* living human being residing *temporarily* inside his or her mother. That's the science of the matter.

- Alcorn, ProLife Answers, 56–57.
- Kaczor, The Ethics of Abortion, 75.
- Ramesh Ponnuru, The Party of Death: The Democrats, the Media, the Courts, and the Disregard for Human Life (Washington, DC: Regnery, 2006), 77.

Pro-Choice Argument #8

A FETUS DOES NOT HAVE RIGHTS UNTIL IT IS "VIABLE"—
UNTIL IT CAN LIVE INDEPENDENTLY.

FIRST REBUTTAL

"Viability" is a purely arbitrary determinate of rights. How is *temporary dependency on another for life* grounds for someone killing you? How about a man in a temporary coma? He's fully dependent on feeding tubes, ventilators, intravenous lines, and twenty-four-hour medical care. Does he also forfeit his right to life when he finds himself in this condition?

- Kaczor, *The Ethics of Abortion*, 70.
- Alcorn, *ProLife Answers*, 85–86.
- Francis J. Beckwith, *Politically Correct Death: Answering the Arguments for Abortion Rights* (Ada, MI: Baker Books, 1993), 99–101.

SECOND REBUTTAL

"Viability" is arbitrary because it is not a fixed point in time. It's dependent not only on the stage of the unborn child's development but also on the medical technology available to the child if he or she were to be born at that minute. What was not viable in 1973 is now viable in 2021. How can any assessment of whether the unborn is "alive," "human," a "person," or "possessing rights" depend on the technology in your particular town or the year you were conceived?

- Alcorn, ProLife Answers, 85.
- Beckwith, Politically Correct Death, 99–101.
- Ponnuru, The Party of Death, 206.

THIRD REBUTTAL

In the end, if it's not a life, you can do whatever you want with it. But if it is a life, you can't do anything to it.

- Live Action News, "Ben Shapiro Destroys Argument that a 'Fetus' Isn't a Human Life," Save the Storks, September 18, 2017, https://savethestorks.com/2017/09/ben-shapiro-destroys-argument-fetus-isnt-human-life/.

FOURTH REBUTTAL

"Imagine that a woman is pregnant in New York City and she has a viable fetus. She is 22 weeks pregnant. If she gets on a plane and she flies to Bangladesh—guess what? That human fetus is no longer viable because viability in Bangladesh doesn't occur until about 35 weeks. So let's just assume she's hanging out in Bangladesh, she doesn't like it very much, so she decides that she's going to come back to New York City. Are we actually going to suggest that she had a 'person' there in her uterus in New York City, a 'non-person' in Bangladesh, who, when returning to the United States of America, became a 'person' for the second time? It is absolutely absurd."

- Mike Adams, PhD, quoted in Frank Camp, "Watch: Professor Rebuts Three Pro-Abortion Arguments, Notes A 'Profound Difference Between' What Is 'Legal' And What Is 'Moral,'" The Daily Wire, March 3, 2019, https://www.dailywire.com/news/watch-professor-rebuts-three-abortion-arguments-frank-camp.

Pro-Choice Argument #9

A FETUS IS NOT A PERSON—AND HAS NO RIGHTS
OR INTRINSIC VALUE—UNTIL IT IS A CERTAIN SIZE,
DEVELOPED TO A CERTAIN LEVEL, OUTSIDE THE UTERUS,
AND INDEPENDENT.

FIRST REBUTTAL

Since when does the size of a human being determine his or her value? Smaller humans have no less a right to life than larger ones. The right to life does not increase with size or age. Otherwise, toddlers and adolescents would have less of a right to live than adults.

- Klusendorf, "Stepping up to Defend Life."
- Horn, Persuasive Pro-Life, 129–35.
- Kaczor, The Ethics of Abortion, 132.
- Alcorn, ProLife Answers, 105.
- Beckwith, Politically Correct Death, 113–14.

SECOND REBUTTAL

Human development is simply a series of progressive stages, including embryo, fetus, infant, adolescent, and adult. These are advancing stages of human development, not advancing stages of intrinsic value. Just as an adolescent doesn't have greater intrinsic value than an infant, an infant has no greater intrinsic value than a fetus.

- Klusendorf, "Stepping up to Defend Life."
- Horn, *Persuasive Pro-Life*, 129–35.
- Kaczor, *The Ethics of Abortion*, 148.
- Alcorn, *ProLife Answers*, 105.
- Beckwith, *Politically Correct Death*, 113–14.

THIRD REBUTTAL

Where you are *located*—in or out of the uterus—does not determine what you are or what your value is. We shouldn't discriminate against anyone because of his or her place of residence. How does a six-inch journey through the birth canal magically confer life or value?

- Klusendorf, "Stepping up to Defend Life."
- Horn, *Persuasive Pro-Life*, 129–35.
- Kaczor, *The Ethics of Abortion*, 50.
- Alcorn, *ProLife Answers*, 59.
- Beckwith, *Politically Correct Death*, 113–14.

FOURTH REBUTTAL

Dependence on another for life is no justification for killing them. Newborns are fully dependent on the adults in their lives, but they don't have less intrinsic value than adults. Should people in comas, stroke victims, or Alzheimer's patients also forfeit their rights to life? Are they no longer "persons" because they're dependent on others? A human's dependency is not grounds for forfeiting one's right to life. Someone's helplessness should motivate us to protect him or her, not to destroy the person.

- Klusendorf, "Stepping up to Defend Life."
- Horn, Persuasive Pro-Life, 129–35.
- Kaczor, The Ethics of Abortion, 132.
- Alcorn, ProLife Answers, 87–89.
- Beckwith, Politically Correct Death, 113–14.

PRO-CHOICE ARGUMENT #10

ABORTION SHOULD BE PERMITTED
UNTIL THE FETUS CAN FEEL PAIN.

FIRST REBUTTAL

Why should the inability of an unborn child to feel pain at a certain stage make the killing of that baby OK? Do you really want to argue that as long as we make sure the killing of people is done without pain, it is somehow acceptable? And what about fully grown adults who suffer from medical conditions where they cannot feel pain? Should these adults also have no right to life?

- Kaczor, The Ethics of Abortion, 41.
- Alcorn, ProLife Answers, 66.
- Horn, Persuasive Pro-Life, 93.

SECOND REBUTTAL

Even if we accepted the "abortion until ability to feel pain" criterion, this would still prohibit all abortions after twenty weeks, since there is universal scientific consensus that the unborn child feels pain at twenty weeks, possibly earlier.

- "Fetal Pain: The Evidence," Doctors on Fetal Pain, updated February 2013, http://www.doctorsonfetalpain.com.
- Ben Shapiro, "Can They Feel Pain?" Facebook video, January 22, 2019, https://www.facebook.com/watch/?v=226062301634625.

"A society will be judged on the basis of how it treats its weakest members; and among the most vulnerable are surely the unborn and the dying."

—POPE ST. JOHN PAUL II

Pro-Choice Argument
#11

AN EMBRYO OR FETUS IS UNAWARE OF ITS OWN
DESTRUCTION, SO IT DOESN'T MATTER.

REBUTTAL

"Awareness of harm" has never been required to make
an act morally wrong. Nor should it. A drunken woman
who passed out at a college frat party might never know
she was raped by three men. Does her lack of "awareness" make the rape acceptable? A morally wrong act
is morally wrong whether or not it is observed or felt.

- Kaczor, The Ethics of Abortion, 76–80, 120.

- Beckwith, Politically Correct Death, 102–3, 106.

- Alcorn, ProLife Answers, 75, 144.

"In order to terminate a pregnancy, you have to still a heartbeat, switch off a developing brain . . . break some bones, and rupture some organs."

—CHRISTOPHER HITCHENS

CATEGORY 2:

A WOMAN'S AUTONOMY

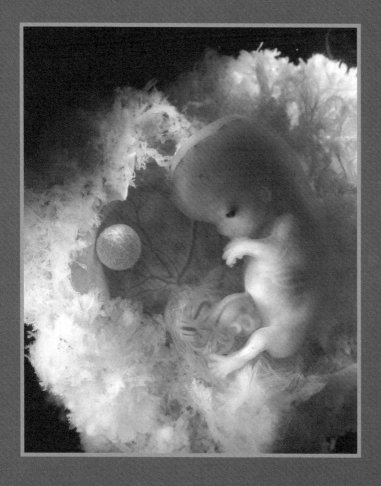

(WEEKS 11–12)

MY BODY, MY CHOICE!

A WOMAN HAS THE RIGHT TO CONTROL HER OWN BODY.

KEEP YOUR LAWS OUT OF MY UTERUS!

FIRST REBUTTAL

I fully support the right of a woman to do whatever she wants with her own body. I just don't believe she has the right to do whatever she wants to someone else's body. A pregnancy always involves two bodies, sometimes more.

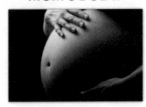

MOM'S BODY:

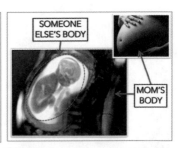

SOMEONE ELSE'S BODY

MOM'S BODY

- Daniel Payne, "Here's a Primer on Pro-Life Responses to Common Counter-Arguments," The Federalist, January 30, 2017, https://thefederalist.com/2017/01/30/heres-primer-pro-life-responses-common-counter-arguments/.
- Kaczor, The Ethics of Abortion, 184–86.

- Alcorn, ProLife Answers, 99.
- Beckwith, Politically Correct Death, 124–25.

SECOND REBUTTAL

There's overwhelming scientific consensus that an embryo or fetus is not part of a woman's body. Instead, it is a genetically distinct, living human being—another "body." So, a woman is free to do whatever she wants to her own body, but she is not free to inflict harm on someone else's body. As they say, "Your right to swing your fist ends just before it touches my nose."

- Alcorn, ProLife Answers, 56–57.
- Kaczor, The Ethics of Abortion, 75.
- Ponnuru, The Party of Death, 77.
- Payne, "Here's a Primer on Pro-Life Responses."

Pro-Choice Argument
#15 and #16

A WOMAN HAS A RIGHT TO CHOOSE!

REPRODUCTIVE JUSTICE!

For discussions related to abortion in the case of rape, please see page 72.

...see page 72.

FIRST REBUTTAL

Yes, a woman should always have the right to choose. I agree completely. The choice she has, though, is *not* whether or not to kill her baby; it is *whether or not to have sex in the first place.* When a woman chooses to have sex, she does so with the full knowledge that there's a real possibility that the act may create a new living human being inside her. It's certainly reasonable, then, for society to expect that adult—one who knowingly consented to that risk—to live temporarily with inconvenience—even significant inconvenience—if the only alternative is killing a child.

- Alcorn, ProLife Answers, 107–9.
- Kaczor, The Ethics of Abortion, 173.

SECOND REBUTTAL

I'm also very Pro-Choice—with just *one less choice than* you. I believe you have lots of choices: you can choose abstinence, motherhood, or adoption. I just don't believe you can choose to kill your baby.

- Steven Crowder, "I'm Pro-Life. Change My Mind," November 7, 2017, YouTube video, 1:07:02, https://www.youtube.com/watch?v=OCSZYJywQPM.
- Alcorn, ProLife Answers, 110–13, 121.

THIRD REBUTTAL

You say a woman has a right to choose. To choose what exactly? It's strange that so many who support abortion are afraid to actually use the word. I wonder what they're afraid of. Why don't you just say what you mean: "I want the right to choose to kill my living baby." Does that really sound like a right you want to defend?

- Alexandra Desanctis, "Biden and Harris Celebrate Roe without Saying 'Abortion,'" National Review, January 22, 2021, https://www.nationalreview.com/corner/biden-and-harris-celebrate-roe-without-saying-abortion/.

FOURTH REBUTTAL

I think you're confused about the actual definition of "justice", which is giving each his due. This requires assessing the rights of the involved parties. In the mother's case, the right is to a lifestyle—one free of the burden of carrying an unwanted pregnancy. For the baby, it's the right to not be killed—the actual right to life. And the right to life must always trump lifestyle. What then is reproductive justice? It's putting the actual life of a child before the lifestyle of his or her mother.

Pro-Choice Argument #17

EVEN IF THE UNBORN ARE LIVING HUMAN BEINGS, THEY HAVE FEWER RIGHTS THAN THE MOTHER.

REBUTTAL

The comparison between a baby's rights and a mother's rights requires a discussion of the actual rights we're talking about. We're speaking of a mother's *right to a certain lifestyle* and her temporary inconvenience, versus the baby's *right to live*. These two rights—lifestyle versus life itself—are simply not equal in moral weight. Life always trumps lifestyle.

- Kaczor, The Ethics of Abortion, 178.

- Alcorn, ProLife Answers, 107.

Pro-Choice Argument #18

A WOMAN SHOULD NOT BE REQUIRED TO BE A
HUMAN INCUBATOR.

REBUTTAL

We are not talking about some dystopian fiction where woman are kidnapped and required to be human incubators against their will. We are speaking of women who choose to have sex with the full knowledge that there's a real possibility that it may create a new living human being inside her. It's certainly reasonable, then, for society to expect that woman—one who knowingly consented to that risk—to live temporarily with that inconvenience (even significant inconvenience) if the only alternative is killing a child.

- Kaczor, The Ethics of Abortion, 178.
- Alcorn, ProLife Answers, 107.

"Abortion reflects a profoundly defective anthropology, according to which every individual is sovereign and everybody else we encounter, even our own children, are to be considered first and foremost a threat to that sovereignty....The dependent status of the weak carries with it moral obligations for the strong—indeed, that dependency and obligation to one another are what make us truly human."

—CARL R. TRUEMAN

CATEGORY 3:
ONE SHOULD NEVER IMPOSE THEIR PERSONAL BELIEFS ON OTHERS

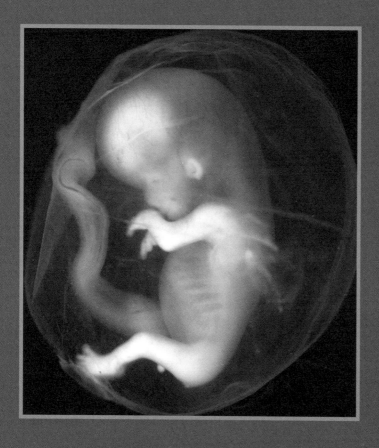

(WEEK 10)

WHO ARE YOU TO IMPOSE YOUR PERSONAL
VALUE SYSTEM ON ME?!

WE ARE ALL FREE TO HAVE OUR OWN OPINIONS
AND MAKE OUR OWN CHOICES.

IF YOU DON'T LIKE ABORTION, THEN DON'T HAVE ONE!

PRO-LIFERS WANT TO IMPOSE THEIR MORALITY ON
EVERYONE ELSE. THEY'RE JUST INTOLERANT.

WE ARE ALL ENTITLED TO OUR OWN MORAL
BELIEF SYSTEMS.

REBUTTAL

That's nonsense. We *all* believe in imposing morality, and we do it every day. On critical moral issues—like rape, child abuse, murder, or theft—we *never* rely on each individual's personal moral code to best guide their actions. We declare to the world that rape and murder are repugnant, immoral, and illegal—and we'll throw you in prison if you dare to rape or kill! That's "imposing morality" and we impose it on every single member of society every single day. So let's not

SPEAKING FOR THE UNBORN

pretend that we don't believe in imposing morality—
every single one of us does.

- Fisher, "How to Stop Any Pro-Choice Argument."
- Beckwith, Politically Correct Death, 81–82.
- Kaczor, The Ethics of Abortion, 218–22.
- Alcorn, ProLife Answers, 110–11.

Pro-Choice Argument #24

I'M PERSONALLY PRO-LIFE, BUT WHO AM I TO IMPOSE MY VIEWS ON OTHERS?

REBUTTAL

On critical moral issues—like slavery, child abuse, rape, or murder—we all have a moral obligation to impose that morality on the rest of the world. These actions should be morally repugnant to every human being. Can you imagine someone saying, "I'm personally anti-slavery, but who am I to impose my view on others? I'd never own a slave, but if you want a slave or two, that's none of my business." Clearly, you and I fully know that we have a *moral obligation to impose* our views about slavery on everyone, everywhere. In fact, not imposing your morality on critical moral issues is, frankly, immoral. Oh, and, by the way, I'm also personally against wife-beating, but . . .

- Paul Stark, "'I'm Personally Pro-Life But' Really Just Means You're Pro-Abortion," LifeNews.com, August 23, 2018, https://www.lifenews.com/2018/08/23/im-personally-pro-life-but-really-just-means-youre-pro-abortion/.

- Alcorn, *ProLife Answers*, 132–36.

- Fisher, "How to Stop Any Pro-Choice Argument."

Pro-Choice Arguments #25 and #26

> KEEP YOUR RELIGION OUT OF MY UTERUS!
>
> KEEP YOUR ROSARIES OFF MY OVARIES!

REBUTTAL

While many of the world's major religions oppose abortion, opposition to abortion need not be based on religion at all. My own opposition to abortion is based on science, the law, reason, morality, social justice, and the visible evidence.

- Fisher, "How to Stop Any Pro-Choice Argument."
- Alcorn, ProLife Answers, 166.
- Kaczor, The Ethics of Abortion, 26.

Pro-Choice Argument
#27

THE VERY PRIVATE DECISION WHETHER OR NOT
TO HAVE AN ABORTION IS BEST LEFT TO A WOMAN
AND HER DOCTOR.

REBUTTAL

The advice or assistance of a physician to commit an act does not change the moral character of that act. An *act that is intrinsically immoral cannot be made moral by the assistance of anyone.* For example, would anyone actually believe that it is OK to drown a three-day-old baby just because a doctor recommended it?

- Alcorn, ProLife Answers, 117–18.
- Horn, Persuasive Pro-Life, 69.

"I just don't believe that being a burden on someone is justification for you killing them."

—Ben Shapiro

Category 4:

Women Shouldn't Have to Bear the Burden and Personal Hardship of an Unwanted Pregnancy

(Week 20)

I JUST CAN'T AFFORD A BABY RIGHT NOW.

HAVING A BABY NOW WOULD DEVASTATE MY CAREER.

I'D HAVE TO QUIT SCHOOL, PUTTING MY
ENTIRE FUTURE AT RISK.

A BABY RIGHT NOW WOULD BE HARMFUL
TO MY OTHER CHILDREN.

FIRST REBUTTAL

Yes, having a baby can be terribly inconvenient, but when did it become OK to kill a living person simply because we feel we can't afford him or her—or because the child might interfere with our personal plans? If it's unacceptable to kill a living baby the minute after she's born, it's also unacceptable to kill her before she's born.

- Fisher, "How to Stop Any Pro-Choice Argument."
- Beckwith, Politically Correct Death, 123–35.
- Horn, Persuasive Pro-Life, 28, 168.

SECOND REBUTTAL

If the unborn is not a living human being, then no justification for abortion is necessary. But if the unborn is a living human being, then no justification is adequate.

- Greg Koukl, "Only One Question," Stand to Reason, February 28, 2013, https://www.str.org/articles/only-one-question#.XPpbIi2ZOg8.

- Stephen Wagner, "What Is It?" Life Media Resources, Vimeo video, 2009, https://vimeo.com/3285507.

THIRD REBUTTAL

Being a burden on someone is never justification for killing them.

- Shapiro, "March for Life Speech."
- Randy Alcorn, "Does a Fetus in the First Trimester Have Value? Ben Shapiro's Answer to a ProChoice College Student," *Eternal Perspective Ministries* (blog), September 27, 2017, https://www.epm.org/blog/2017/Sep/27/fetus-value-ben-shapiro.

FOURTH REBUTTAL

A mother cannot end the life of her unborn child for the same reason that she cannot kill her two-year-old toddler when that child is a hardship. Both are living human beings entitled to a right to live. Just as there are resources in society to help a mother care for her two-year-old during times of hardship, there are also resources available for struggling mothers during pregnancy—crisis pregnancy centers, religious charities, private charities, and government assistance. And we must all work tirelessly to get these resources to all pregnant women in need.

- Fisher, "How to Stop Any Pro-Choice Argument."
- Horn, *Persuasive Pro-Life*, 60–65.

- Greg Koukl, "Trotting Out the Toddler," Stand to Reason, May 29, 2013, https://www.str.org/w/trotting-out-the-toddler.

CATEGORY 5:

YOU ARE JUST ANTI-WOMAN, A MISOGYNIST

(WEEK 16)

Pro-Choice Argument #32

YOU ARE JUST ANTI-WOMAN!

REBUTTAL

I'm not anti-woman; I'm just anti-killing. In fact, since nearly half a million baby girls are aborted each year in the United States, my position is fiercely pro-woman.

- Alcorn, ProLife Answers, 113.

- Leanna Cinquanta, "Pro-Life Is Not Anti-Women's Rights . . . Just Anti-Murder," Leanna Cinquanta (blog), February 4, 2017, https://leannacinquanta.com/pro-life-is-not-anti-womens-rights-just-anti-murder/.

Pro-Choice Arguments
#33, #34, #35, and #36

ABORTION IS SIMPLY A NORMAL PART OF WOMEN'S
HEALTH CARE—A CRITICAL ELEMENT OF WOMEN'S
REPRODUCTIVE HEALTH.

YOU DON'T CARE ABOUT WOMEN'S
REPRODUCTIVE HEALTH!

YOU DON'T CARE ABOUT THE HEALTH, WELFARE,
AND SAFETY OF WOMEN!

YOU'RE A MISOGYNIST!

FIRST REBUTTAL
If your healthcare kills people on purpose, then you're
clearly doing it wrong.

SECOND REBUTTAL
When did lethally injecting a living unborn child, or
tearing it limb from limb and suctioning it from its
mother's womb, become "health care"? Treating the
diabetic is health care. Setting a broken bone is health
care. Performing open-heart surgery is health care.
Killing a living unborn child has nothing to do with
health care.

- Randy Alcorn, "Is Abortion Really a Women's Rights Issue?" chap. 8 in *Why Pro-Life? Caring for the Unborn and Their Mothers* (Peabody, MA: Hendrickson, 2012).

- Timothy M. Jackson, "Why Elective Abortion Can Never Constitute Health Care," The Federalist, January 3, 2018, https://thefederalist.com/2018/01/03/elective-abortion-is-not-healthcare-end-of-story/.

- Ryan Bomberger, "No, Abortion Is Not Health Care. It's #FakeHealth," Life Site News, August 1, 2018, https://www.lifesitenews.com/opinion/no-abortion-is-not-health-care.-its-fakehealth.

THIRD REBUTTAL

Why don't we drop the euphemisms and be clear on what abortion is—as defined by medical textbooks everywhere: *Abortion is the elective killing of an innocent living human being—an unborn child.* And it rarely has anything to do with health care: nearly 95% of all abortions are performed on the *healthy* babies of *healthy* mothers. Abortion is not health care.

- *Merriam-Webster's Collegiate Dictionary*, s.v. "abortion," accessed on August 14, 2021, https://www.merriam-webster.com/dictionary/abortion.

- Mary Szoch, ed., *The Best Pro-Life Arguments for Secular Audiences* (Washington, DC: Family Research Council, 2021), https://www.frc.org/brochure/the-best-pro-life-arguments-for-secular-audiences.

- "When Human Life Begins," American College of Pediatricians.

- *The American Heritage Medical Dictionary*, s.v. "life."

- Moore, Persaud, and Torchia, *The Developing Human*, 11.

- Schoenwolf et al., *Larsen's Human Embryology*, 2, 14.

PRO-CHOICE ARGUMENT
#37

FIRST REBUTTAL

First of all, let's be very clear: no major voice in the Pro-Life movement argues that a mother must risk her life to carry her pregnancy to term. The life of the mother is always prioritized in the case of true maternal danger.

But there is a fallacy that we need to address: abortions to "save the life" of the mother during the third trimester (Weeks 29–40). The fact is, there is simply never a situation where abortion is required to save the life of the mother during the third trimester. In those very rare cases where the mother's life is at risk in the third trimester, the baby can simply be delivered. In fact, the delivery of a live baby is much faster than a late-term abortion, which usually takes at least forty-eight hours. And since babies as young as twenty-one weeks are now able to survive premature delivery, there is never any justification for killing a baby during this time period.

And let's remember, nearly 95% of all abortions are performed on the *healthy* babies of *healthy* mothers.

- Alcorn, *ProLife Answers*, 221.
- Kaczor, *The Ethics of Abortion*, 203.
- Cassy Fiano-Chesser, "Watch: Abortion Is Never Medically Necessary, and It's Not Health Care," Live Action News, December 22, 2018, https://www.liveaction.org/news/abortion-never-medically-health-care/.
- Szoch, *The Best Pro-Life Arguments*.
- Lawrence B. Finer et al., "Reasons US Women Have Abortions: Quantitative and Qualitative Perspectives," *Perspectives on Sexual and Reproductive Health* 37, no. 5 (2005): 113–14.

SECOND REBUTTAL

Abortion *to save a mother's life* was legal *before* Roe v. Wade and *will remain legal* now that Roe has been overturned. The life of the mother is *always* protected by the Pro-Life movement. For example, even the most vocal Pro-Life advocates believe that treating an ectopic pregnancy is absolutely necessary, as it endangers the life of the mother.

- Alcorn, *ProLife Answers*, 222.

THIRD REBUTTAL

It is important to remember that the "health" of the mother is a very different thing than the "life" of the mother. Currently, the legal definition for the health of the mother includes the very vague assessment of "emotional well-being," which permits any mother who feels "distressed" about being pregnant to qualify for an abortion at *any* time. This is a far cry from exceptions for the life of the mother.

- Horn, Persuasive Pro-Life, 37–38.
- Doe v. Bolton, 410 U.S. 179 (1972), www.loc.gov /item/ usrep410179/.
- Beckwith, Politically Correct Death, 31–34.
- Alcorn, ProLife Answers, 222.

"To sin by silence when they should protest, makes cowards of men."

—ABRAHAM LINCOLN

Pro-Choice Argument #38

NOTE: *Whenever discussing rape and abortion, always be mindful that the person you are speaking with may have been the victim of this horrendous crime. On this delicate issue, then, always be gentle, compassionate and respectful.*

FIRST REBUTTAL

The extremely rare cases of rape and incest are among the most common arguments made in support of abortion. It's an attempt to take the exceptional case and say it somehow applies to all cases. That's just faulty logic, as we never make laws based on the exceptional case. If rape and incest—which account for less than 0.5% of all abortions—are your argument for the right to abortion, can I assume you would be willing to join me in opposing the other 99.5% of cases?

- Ben Shapiro, "Ben Shapiro Torches Arrogant Leftist in Epic Battle over Abortion," Young America's Foundation, July 7, 2018, YouTube video, 2:19, https://www.youtube.com/watch?v=BIQRIOLbGqg&frags=pl%2Cwn.
- Fisher, "How to Stop Any Pro-Choice Argument."
- Kaczor, *The Ethics of Abortion*, 195.
- Alcorn, *ProLife Answers*, 231, 236.

SECOND REBUTTAL

The violence of abortion is no solution for the violence of rape. Where else do we solve one horrible thing with another equally horrible thing? A child is a child regardless of the circumstances of its conception.

- Alcorn, ProLife Answers, 231–36.
- Horn, Persuasive Pro-Life, 167, 196.
- Kaczor, The Ethics of Abortion, 195.
- Beckwith, Politically Correct Death, 68–72.

THIRD REBUTTAL

The calculus is simple. If it's not a human life, you can do whatever you want with it. But if it is a human life, you can't do anything to it.

- Live Action News, "Ben Shapiro Destroys Argument."

Pro-Choice Arguments #39, #40, and #41

YOU MEN SHOULD MIND YOUR OWN BUSINESS!

ABORTION IS PURELY A WOMEN'S ISSUE.

NO UTERUS? NO OPINION!

FIRST REBUTTAL

Nonsense. Abortion is a human issue, not a gender issue. Facts, logic, reason, and compassion have no anatomy. Whether men or women support these views is no more relevant than whether they're supported by blacks or whites. To believe otherwise is simply bigotry and sexism. You didn't have to be black to oppose slavery or a Jew to oppose Nazis. As Martin Luther King Jr. said regarding moral issues, "A man dies when he refuses to stand up for justice."

- Alcorn, ProLife Answers, 286.
- Michael Robinson, "No Uterus, No Opinion? Should Men Have a Voice on Abortion?" LifeNews.com, March 1, 2019, https://www.lifenews.com/2019/03/01/no-uterus-no-opinion-should-men-have-a-voice-on-abortion/.
- Ethan Lucky and Skyler Lee, "'No Uterus, No Opinion?' Why Men Must Speak Out against Abortion," Human Defense Initiative, May 29, 2018, https://humandefense.com/no-uterus-no-opinion/.

- Martin Luther King Jr., "Speaks from the Pulpit on Courage" (transcript of speech, Selma, AL, March 8, 1965), accessed October 11, 2021, http://faculty.etsu.edu/history/documents/mlkselma.htm.

SECOND REBUTTAL

Abortion is a human issue, not a gender issue. My personal identity has nothing to do with what is right or wrong. I don't surrender the right to take a stand on moral or political issues simply because of my skin color or gender. To suggest otherwise is racist, sexist, and bigoted.

- Ben Shapiro, "Ben Shapiro on Abortion: Evil Is Still Evil Regardless of Identity Politics," January 25, 2018, YouTube video, 2:19, https://www.youtube.com/watch?v=047DSK2mTeo&frags=pl%2Cwn.
- Alcorn, ProLife Answers, 286.
- Robinson, "No Uterus, No Opinion?"
- Lucky and Lee, "No Uterus, No Opinion?"

THIRD REBUTTAL

I would echo the sentiments of both Martin Luther King, Jr. and Abraham Lincoln—that it would be cowardly and immoral to permit anyone to silence you on critical moral issues based on your skin color, your religion, or your sex. And to suggest otherwise is racist, sexist, and bigoted.

Pro-Choice Argument #42

THE PRO-LIFE MOVEMENT IS JUST ANOTHER EXAMPLE OF MEN SUBJUGATING WOMEN.

FIRST REBUTTAL

That's nonsense. First, opinion polls show that men are actually *less* opposed to abortion than women. Second, the overwhelming majority of Pro-Life workers and volunteers are *women*, not men. Third, the leader of nearly every national Pro-Life group is a woman! So the notion that the Pro-Life movement is a weapon used by men is pure fiction.

- Kaczor, *The Ethics of Abortion*, 8.
- Lydia Saad, "Americans Divided over Abortion Debate: Similar Percentages Call Themselves Pro-Choice and Pro-Life," Gallup, May 18, 1999, https://news.gallup.com/poll/3847/americans-divided-over-abortion-debate.aspx.
- Alcorn, *ProLife Answers*, 250–52.

SECOND REBUTTAL

That's a demonstrably false statement—debunked by even a cursory review of the facts. The Pro-Life movement is led by *women*, not men (2021):

- **March for Life:** Jeanne Mancini

- **Susan B. Anthony List:** Marjorie Dannenfelser
- **Live Action:** Lila Rose
- **And Then There Were None:** Abby Johnson
- **Students for Life:** Kristan Hawkins
- **Americans United for Life:** Catherine Glenn Foster
- **New Wave Feminists:** Destiny Herndon-De La Rosa
- **Right to Life:** Carol Tobias

- Taryn Oesch DeLong, "Inside Look: Women Leading the Pro-Life Movement," April 20, 2020, https://www.femcatholic.com/post/facing-goliath-the-women-leading-the-pro-life-movement.
- Ashley E. McGuire, "Pro-Life Movement Has Always Been Driven by Women," The Hill, January 21, 2016, https://thehill.com/blogs/congress-blog/civil-rights/266470-pro-life-movement-has-always-been-driven-by-women.

THIRD REBUTTAL

Men are at their best when they exercise deep loyalties to women and children—when they take responsibility to protect and defend them. When men violate these duties, they are at their worst, becoming either abusers or cowards.

- George Gilder, *Men and Marriage*, 5th ed. (Gretna, LA: Pelican, 2008).

PRO-CHOICE ARGUMENT #43

> IF ABORTION IS MADE ILLEGAL, THOUSANDS OF
> WOMEN WILL DIE IN BACK-ALLEY AND CLOTHES-
> HANGER ABORTIONS.

FIRST REBUTTAL

That's a fiction based on the false testimony of former abortionist Bernard Nathanson, who once said that "5,000–10,000 women died of back-alley abortions each year prior to Roe." He later admitted that he completely made up this number. In the years prior to Roe v. Wade, the actual number of abortion deaths of the mother was about 250 a year. Also before Roe, 90% of all illegal abortions were performed by physicians in back offices with surgical instruments, not in back alleys with clothes hangers. Where abortion is now once again made illegal, the small percentage of women seeking to break the law would resume this same "back office" medical practice. So "thousands of women dying from back-alley abortions and clothes hangers" is pure fiction.

- Alcorn, ProLife Answers, 173–77.
- Szoch, The Best Pro-Life Arguments.
- Kaczor, The Ethics of Abortion, 198.

SECOND REBUTTAL

"We must not legalize procedures that kill the innocent just to make the killing process less hazardous. . . . We don't try to make kidnapping or child abuse safe and legal. If abortion kills children, our goal should not be to make it as safe and legal as possible, but to provide alternatives and legal restrictions that help avoid it in the first place."

- Alcorn, ProLife Answers, 177–78.

THIRD REBUTTAL

We know from other countries that restricting abortion does not cause an increase in maternal deaths. Ireland and Malta, for example, have some of the lowest maternal mortality rates in the world despite their tight abortion restrictions. And Poland experienced a documented *decrease* in maternal deaths when abortion was made illegal.

- Maternal Mortality in 2005: Estimates Developed by WHO, UNICEF, UNFPA and The World Bank (Geneva, CH: World Health Organization, 2007), http://www.who.int/whosis/mme_2005.pdf.

- Kaczor, The Ethics of Abortion, 202.

- Alcorn, ProLife Answers, 174–75.

CATEGORY 6:

ABORTION EMPOWERS WOMEN

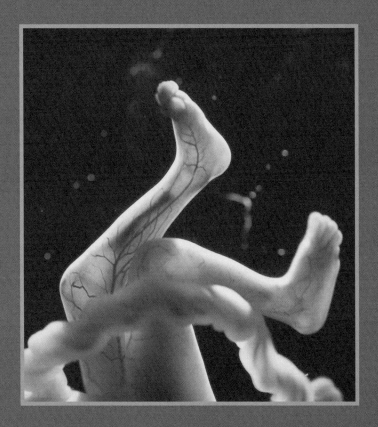

(WEEKS 15–16)

PRO-CHOICE ARGUMENTS #44, #45, AND #46

ABORTION EMPOWERS WOMEN.

ABORTION IS IN THE BEST INTEREST OF WOMEN'S
PHYSICAL AND MENTAL WELL-BEING.

ABORTION IS ESSENTIAL IN ORDER FOR WOMEN
TO HAVE EQUALITY WITH MEN.

FIRST REBUTTAL

Abortion has never empowered women. It has empowered men, though—empowered them to use women for sexual pleasure, without any long-term consequences. Abortion has normalized men's ability to use, exploit, manipulate, abuse, and abandon women. And you say this empowers women?

- Ryan Bomberger, "'Reverend' Rob Schenck's Pro-Abortion Pitch Is Pathetic," Townhall, June 8, 2019, https://townhall.com/columnists/ryanbomberger/2019/06/08/reverend-rob-schencks-pro-abortion-pitch-is-pathetic-n2547379.

- Matt Walsh, "Why Sexist Deadbeat Men Love Abortion," The Daily Wire, April 24, 2019, https://www.dailywire.com/news/46379/walsh-why-sexist-deadbeat-men-love-abortion-matt-walsh.

SECOND REBUTTAL

What actually empowers women is to not see children and fertility as threats. It is a perversion of feminism to believe that women and children are natural enemies. Women shouldn't have to kill their children to achieve their dreams or achieve full participation in society. If a pregnant woman or mother can't participate in society, then something is wrong with society, not with their fertility—that's a true feminist response.

- Lila Rose, "Women don't need to kill their children to pursue the dreams, goals, and careers that they want," Facebook, September 5, 2018, https://www.facebook.com/lilagracerose/posts/women-dont-need-to-kill-their-children-to-pursue-the-dreams-goals-and-careers-th/10156802063183000/.

- Szoch, The Best Pro-Life Arguments.

- Kaczor, The Ethics of Abortion, 176.

- Alcorn, ProLife Answers, 192.

Pro-Choice Argument #47

WHY SHOULD ONLY MEN BE ABLE TO ENGAGE IN SEX WITHOUT LIFE-ALTERING CONSEQUENCES?

REBUTTAL

The feminist movement wasn't wrong when it said that men were acting like pigs. They were wrong, though, in saying that the solution to this sad fact is for women to *also* act like pigs. Women's equality shouldn't mean emulating the very worst and most damaging qualities of men. So we have thrown out traditional values—like the notion that sex ought to be connected to love and marriage—so that sex is now just another bodily function, like eating. And this dramatic shift has damaged all of us—women, children, men, and families.

- Ben Shapiro, "How Feminism Ruined Marriage," The Daily Wire, October 5, 2018, YouTube video, 4:45, https:// www.youtube.com/ watch?v=ILUkWyGfuJA&frags=pl%2Cwn.

- Ben Shapiro, "Marriage Was Set-Up to Protect Women Because Men are Pigs," September 17, 2019, https:// twitter.com/yaf/status/1173952244435304448?lang=en.

"Abortion and racism are both symptoms of a fundamental human error. The error is thinking that when someone stands in the way of our wants, we can justify getting that person out of our lives. Abortion and racism stem from the same poisonous root: selfishness."

—ALVEDA KING

CATEGORY 7:

ABORTION IS BEST FOR SOCIETY AND BEST FOR UNWANTED BABIES

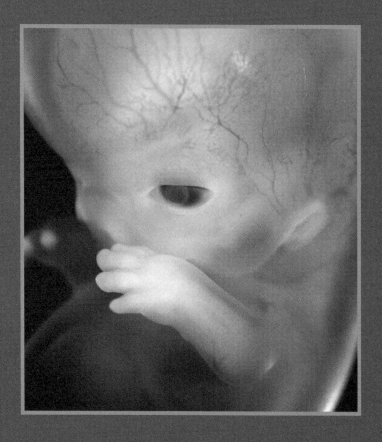

(WEEK 10)

Pro-Choice Arguments #48 and #49

EVERY CHILD SHOULD BE WANTED.

BETTER FOR A BABY TO BE ABORTED THAN TO BE UNWANTED, UNLOVED, AND A BURDEN.

FIRST REBUTTAL

It isn't an act of love or fairness or compassion to kill someone simply because they're unwanted. How can killing an unborn child—dismembering him while in the womb—ever be for his own benefit? The most uncompassionate, unkind, and unloving thing you can do to a child is to kill him.

- Alcorn, ProLife Answers, 139, 141.
- Kaczor, The Ethics of Abortion, 193–94.
- Horn, Persuasive Pro-Life, 190.

SECOND REBUTTAL

We need to be clear about the terms we are using here. An "unwanted pregnancy" is not the same thing as an "unwanted child." Currently, an estimated two million families are waiting to adopt children. So many of these "unwanted pregnancies" are, in fact, carrying "wanted children."

- "How Many Couples Are Waiting to Adopt a Baby?" American Adoptions, accessed August 14, 2021, https://www.americanadoptions.com/pregnant/ waiting_adoptive_families.

- Alcorn, ProLife Answers, 139–40.

- Horn, Persuasive Pro-Life, 95–96, 298.

- Kaczor, The Ethics of Abortion, 43–45.

Pro-Choice Argument #50

BETTER TO BE ABORTED THAN TO END UP IN THE UNHAPPY FOSTER-CARE SYSTEMS OF MANY STATES.

REBUTTAL

What you are really saying is that it's better to eliminate the sufferer than to eliminate the suffering. Instead of improving foster care and the adoption process, we should just kill the child. How did killing a child become an act of kindness?

- Amanda Prestigiacomo, "Watch: 'Students for Life' President Demolishes Common Pro-Abortion Talking Point from Feminist," The Daily Wire, May 29, 2019, https://www.dailywire.com/news/watch-students-life-president-demolishes-common-amanda-prestigiacomo.

SPEAKING FOR THE UNBORN

Worldviews

Close One: This Baby Was Almost Born Into Poverty But His Mother Killed Him In The Nick Of Time

May 16th, 2019 · BabylonBee.com

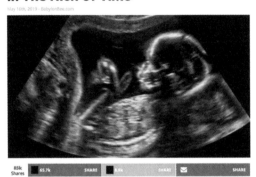

85k Shares	65.7k	SHARE	8.5k	SHARE	✉	SHARE

Talk about a close call: this baby was almost born into poverty, but his mother killed him just before the cutoff for abortion in their state. With literally just a few days to spare, she ended his life, saving him from living a life that isn't always perfect.

Pro-Choice Argument
#51

IT'S BETTER TO HAVE AN ABORTION THAN TO BRING A
SIGNIFICANTLY HANDICAPPED OR DEFORMED CHILD INTO
THE WORLD, BECAUSE THEIR LIVES WOULD BE SAD
AND LIMITED—AND THEY WOULD BE A TERRIBLE
BURDEN ON OTHERS.

FIRST REBUTTAL

So, you're making an argument for *eugenics*—improving the species and society by eliminating undesirable traits. That's a decision you might want to rethink, because it puts you in the company of groups you would *never* want to be associated with—like Nazis and the Ku Klux Klan. They also wanted to eliminate "inferior" people and those that might be a burden on others. And where does eugenics stop? Are we—are you—ready to eliminate those unborn, who through genetic testing, we know may have a low IQ or will likely become diabetic? All human beings have inherent dignity and it's simply not our role to decide who deserves to live or die. I think we should leave such callous and cold-hearted statements to the Nazis and the KKK.

- Kaczor, The Ethics of Abortion, 191–93.
- Fisher, "How to Stop Any Pro-Choice Argument."

- Horn, *Persuasive Pro-Life*, 196–98.
- Alcorn, *ProLife Answers*, 148–49.

SECOND REBUTTAL

Abortion for deformity or severe handicap accounts for only a small minority of abortions. Nearly 95% of abortions are performed on the *healthy* babies of *healthy* mothers. So arguing for sweeping, unrestricted abortion rights based on this argument is faulty logic.

- Szoch, *The Best Pro-Life Arguments*.
- Finer et al., "Reasons US Women Have Abortions," 113–14.
- Alcorn, *ProLife Answers*, 236.

THIRD REBUTTAL

The majority of handicapped children are happy and glad to be alive. John Merrick, the severely handicapped "Elephant Man," said it best: "I am happy every hour of the day. My life is full because I know I am loved." Did his life have so little value that he should not have been permitted to be born? He thought his life was very worthwhile.

- Patrick D. Odum, "A Child of God: Who Are You?" Heart Light, August 8, 2004, https://www.heartlight.org/articles/200408/20040808_childofgod.html.

FOURTH REBUTTAL

Let's be honest. When we kill a handicapped child in the womb, we really aren't doing it for his own good. We're doing it for what we perceive to be our own good. We are never protecting a child by killing her. We are only trying to protect ourselves.

- Alcorn, ProLife Answers, 224–26.

FIFTH REBUTTAL

Do you know what group of people most disagree with this argument? People with disabilities, and their parents. Those with disabilities don't like it when people tell them that their lives are not worth living. They don't like it when people tell them that ending their lives is the most compassionate thing someone could do for them. They and their parents would tell you that that's the least compassionate act they could ever imagine.

- Angelo Stagnaro, "22 Ways to Respond to Common Abortion Questions," Catholic Education Resource Center, 2019, https://www.catholiceducation.org/en/controversy/abortion/22-ways-to-respond-to-common-abortion-questions.html.

Pro-Choice Argument
#52

ABORTION IS BEST FOR SOCIETY BECAUSE
IT HELPS DECREASE UNWED BIRTH RATES,
CHILD ABUSE, AND CRIME.

REBUTTAL

This is simply untrue. Legalizing abortion has done nothing to reduce unwed births, child abuse, or crime. To the contrary, all have significantly increased since Roe. For example, The National Center on Child Abuse and Neglect has demonstrated that child abuse and neglect have increased over 1,000% since Roe. Unwed births for black children have skyrocketed to 73%. So if decreasing rates of unwed births, child abuse, and crime are your arguments for abortion, you might want to reconsider your position.

- Alcorn, ProLife Answers, 143–44.

- Michael J. New, "Abortion Promises Unfulfilled," Public Discourse, January 23, 2013, https://www. thepublicdiscourse.com/2013/01/7630/.

- Robert VerBruggen, "Trends in Unmarried Childbearing Point to a Coming Apart," Institute for Family Studies, February 20, 2018, https://ifstudies.org/blog/trends-in-unmarried-childbearing-point-to-a-coming-apart.

Pro-Choice Argument #53

RESTRICTING ABORTION IS UNFAIR TO THE POOR AND
MINORITIES, WHO NEED IT THE MOST.

FIRST REBUTTAL

Let's be clear: abortion advocates are not worried about helping the poor or minorities, but they are happy to help them abort their children. In fact, Planned Parenthood, the most prolific killer of the unborn, places the majority of its abortion centers in minority neighborhoods. And its founder, Margaret Sanger, was an outspoken racist who wanted to eliminate "indiscriminate breeding" by minorities, whom she considered "human weeds." And her plan has worked remarkably well: abortion is now the number-one killer of black lives in America—more than heart disease, cancer, and gun violence combined.

- Alcorn, ProLife Answers, 146–50.
- Margaret Sanger, The Pivot of Civilization (New York: Brentano's, 1922), 176.
- Arthur Goldberg, "Abortion's Devastating Impact Upon Black Americans," Public Discourse, February 11, 2019, https://www.thepublicdiscourse.com/2019/02/48594/.

SECOND REBUTTAL

Let me tell you about Planned Parenthood and minorities: Planned Parenthood was founded by a proud racist, Margaret Sanger, who wanted to eliminate "indiscriminate breeding" by minorities, whom she called "human weeds." Her goal was to decrease the black and minority populations, and she actually advocated for the killing of babies. As she famously said in 1920, "The most merciful thing that the large family does to one of its infant members is to kill it." Planned Parenthood has faithfully pursued Sanger's dreams, as the majority of babies now being disposed of are poor and dark skinned. That's Planned Parenthood.

- Alcorn, ProLife Answers, 146–50.
- Sanger, Woman and the New Race (New York: Eugenics Publishing Company, 1920).
- Goldberg, "Abortion's Devastating Impact."
- Steven W. Mosher, "The Repackaging of Margaret Sanger," The Wall Street Journal, May 5, 1997, https://www.wsj.com/articles/SB862769009690799000.

Politics

Planned Parenthood Distances Themselves From Margaret Sanger By Continuing Her Legacy

April 24th, 2021 - BabylonBee.com

5.6k Shares   4.3k   SHARE   575   SHARE   ✉   SHARE

NEW YORK, NY—Planned Parenthood's newest CEO Alexis McGill Johnson has recently made the decision to distance the organization from their racist, eugenicist founder Margaret Sanger.

Pro-Choice Argument #54

ABORTION IS AN IMPORTANT METHOD OF POPULATION
CONTROL IN OUR OVERCROWDED WORLD.

REBUTTAL

Even if we agreed that we have an overpopulation problem, killing off a segment of the population would never be an acceptable solution. Solutions based on killing innocent human beings are never OK.

- Alcorn, ProLife Answers, 153.

- Shapiro, "March for Life Speech."

- Kaczor, The Ethics of Abortion, 47.

CATEGORY 8:

MISCELLANEOUS ARGUMENTS

Pro-Choice Argument #55

THE RECENT DOBBS SUPREME COURT DECISION IS AN OUTRAGE, UNFAIRLY AND RECKLESSLY DISCARDING FIFTY YEARS OF LEGAL PRECEDENT! FOR FIFTY YEARS, WOMEN HAVE HAD THE RIGHT TO ABORTION UNDER ROE V. WADE. YOU JUST CAN'T INVALIDATE FIFTY YEARS OF LEGAL RIGHTS!

REBUTTAL

The Supreme Court has repeatedly held that "bad precedent is no precedent," and we should be thankful that there are established criteria for overturning bad precedents. If not, slavery would still be legal; denying women the right to vote would still be legal; segregated schools would still be legal; "separate but equal" public restrooms and water fountains would still be legal. Thankfully, these horrific practices were overturned. Good people must seek justice for everyone, including the unborn. Overturning legal precedent and amending the Constitution to reflect our advancing understanding of morality, science, and humanity are as American as apple pie.

- Fisher, "How to Stop Any Pro-Choice Argument."
- Alcorn, *ProLife Answers*, 116, 135.
- Ed Grabianowski, "10 Overturned Supreme Court Cases," How Stuff Works, November 10, 2010, https://money.howstuffworks.com/10-overturned-supreme-court-cases.htm.

Pro-Choice Argument #56

WHERE ABORTION IS NOW PROHIBITED, YOU WILL BE INCARCERATING DESPERATE WOMEN WHO MIGHT SEEK NOW-ILLEGAL ABORTIONS. HOW COULD YOU BE THAT CRUEL AND INHUMANE?

REBUTTAL

While breaking the law—especially laws preventing the taking of innocent human life—is certainly grounds for prosecution, *not a single major voice in the Pro-Life movement advocates for the prosecution of women seeking illegal abortions.* There is overwhelming consensus in the Pro-Life movement that only abortionists performing illegal abortions will be prosecuted in states where abortion is made illegal.

- Ben Shapiro, "Ben Shapiro Shreds Pro-Choice Argument 2019," People Choice, February 13, 2019, YouTube video, 17:31, https://www.youtube.com/watch?v=KQ7h0-kq-kU&frags=pl%2Cwn.=.

- David French, "No, Georgia's Heartbeat Bill Won't Imprison Women Who Have Abortions," National Review, May 11, 2019, https://www.nationalreview.com/corner/georgia-heartbeat-bill-will-not-imprison-women-who-have-abortions/.

Pro-Choice Argument #57

REBUTTAL

Simply because some people will break a law is not an argument against the existence of that law. Rape is illegal in the United States, yet this crime is committed daily. Does the fact that rape is still committed mean there should be no laws against rape?

- Alcorn, ProLife Answers, 157.
- Beckwith, Politically Correct Death, 170.

PRO-CHOICE ARGUMENT
#58

REBUTTAL

My personal opinion on contraception is irrelevant to this debate, and the Pro-Life movement does not advocate prohibiting the use of non-abortive contraceptives. We just don't believe in killing living human babies.

- William Saletan, "Do Pro-Lifers Oppose Birth Control?" Slate, January 15, 2014, https://slate.com/news-and-politics/2014/01/do-pro-lifers-oppose-birth-control-polls-say-no.html.

- "Contraception," Students for Life of America, accessed August 16, 2021, https://studentsforlife.org/contraception/.

PRO-CHOICE ARGUMENT
#59

YOU PRO-LIFERS ONLY CARE ABOUT BABIES WHILE THEY
ARE INSIDE THE UTERUS! ONCE THEY ARE BORN, YOU
CONSERVATIVES DON'T CARE FOR THE POOR AND NEEDY.

FIRST REBUTTAL

What makes you think that Conservatives and Pro-Life
advocates care less for the needy than Liberals and
Pro-Choicers? Did you know that Conservatives give a
greater percentage of their income and volunteer more
of their time to the needy than those who identify as
Liberal or Pro-Choice? Now, you might believe that
Liberal social policies are better for the poor than Conservative policies—and that's a legitimate debate to
have. But it's both arrogant and inaccurate to simply
claim that Liberals and Pro-Choicers—who donate less
of their time and money to the poor—care more for
them than Conservatives.

- Nicholas Kristof, "Bleeding Heart Tightwads," New
  York Times, December 20, 2008, https://www.nytimes.
  com/2008/12/21/opinion/21kristof.html.

- Thomas Sowell, "Who Really Cares?" National Review,
  November 28, 2006, https://www.nationalreview.
  com/2006/11/who-really-cares-thomas-sowell/.

- Alcorn, ProLife Answers, 245–50.

- Horn, Persuasive Pro-Life, 216–19.

SECOND REBUTTAL

This is untrue—and statistics regarding adoption are evidence of this falsehood. As I'm sure you know, a large percentage of Pro-Life advocates tend to be religious, predominantly Christian. And Christians are twice as likely to adopt than the general population. Catholics are three times as likely to adopt than the general population, and Evangelicals five times more likely. These are facts that prove the Pro-Life movement is pro-life for all children. So claiming that Pro-Life advocates don't care about babies after they are born is nonsense.

- Russell Moore, "Trump Reverses Obama's Anti-Religious Decree," Wall Street Journal, November 3, 2019, https:// www.wsj.com/articles/trump-reverses-obamas-anti-christian-decree-11572813718.

THIRD REBUTTAL

Can we all do more? Absolutely. We all must do more for expectant mothers who find themselves in a tough spot. All of us—Conservatives, Moderates, and Liberals. And we Pro-Lifers must always remind ourselves that we cannot limit our efforts to the banning of abortion. We must also be strong advocates for all mothers—because "abortion is not a sign that women are free, but a sign that they are desperate." We need to make sure that pregnant mothers know that the Pro-Life movement is on their side!

- Frederica Mathewes-Green, "Abortion: Women's Rights and Wrongs," Frederica.com (blog), January 1, 2000, http://frederica.com/writings/abortion-womens-rights-and-wrongs.html.

"I do not believe the promises of the Declaration of Independence are just for the strong, the independent, the healthy. They are for everyone— including unborn children."

—GEORGE W. BUSH

Pro-Choice Argument #60

WE ARE A DEMOCRACY, AND THE MAJORITY OF AMERICANS SUPPORT ABORTION!

FIRST REBUTTAL

This might come as a surprise to you but polling consistently shows that the majority of Americans believes there should be *greater* restrictions on abortion, not fewer.

- 75% believe in no abortions after Week 12. (This includes 92% of Republicans, 78% of Independents, 60% of Democrats, and 61% who identify *as* Pro-Choice!)

- A majority opposes any taxpayer funding of abortion (54% to only 39%).

- Marist Poll and Knights of Columbus, "Americans' Opinions on Abortion," Life News, January 2019, https://lifenews-wpengine.netdna-ssl.com/wp-content/uploads/2019/01/2019MartistAbortionPoll.pdf.
- Alcorn, *ProLife Answers*, 159–61.

SECOND REBUTTAL

What is alarming is that the leaders of the Pro-Choice movement have little regard for the actual will of the people—not even the will of the average abortion supporter! For example, the New York Senate has now legalized abortion up until the moment of birth, despite 69% of registered New York Democratic voters opposing that same law. (Even 44% of Pro-Choice New Yorkers oppose this law!)

- "Poll Finds Two-Thirds of New Yorkers Oppose Late-Term Abortion," Catholic News Agency, March 29, 2019, https://www.catholicnewsagency.com/news/40909/poll-finds-two-thirds-of-new-yorkers-oppose-late-term-abortion.

- "44% of Pro-Choice Voters Oppose NY Abortion Law in Their State," Rasmussen Reports, February 7, 2019, http://www.rasmussenreports.com/public_content/politics/current_events/abortion/44_of_pro_choice_voters_oppose_ny_abortion_law_in_their_state.

THIRD REBUTTAL

A "majority of Americans supporting some form of abortion" makes abortion neither moral nor justifiable; it only makes it popular—and perhaps only for the time being. The subjugation of blacks and women used to be quite popular as well—and no one would ever consider those evils to be moral or justifiable. We should never confuse popular opinion with morality.

- Avery Foley, "Is Morality Determined by Its Popularity," Answers In Genesis. October 13, 2017, https://answersingenesis.org/morality/is-morality-determined-by-its-popularity/.

PRO-CHOICE ARGUMENT #61

PLANNED PARENTHOOD DOES MORE FOR
WOMEN'S HEALTH AND SOCIETY THAN ANY
PRO-LIFE GROUP EVER DID.

FIRST REBUTTAL

Planned Parenthood would very much like the public to believe that its main concern is women's heath, and it spends huge sums of money trying to persuade the public that it does. But the truth is that *Planned Parenthood exists to perform abortions*, as its most recent President recently admitted, "Our core mission is providing, protecting, and expanding access to abortion and reproductive health care." So if you're actually concerned about women's health care and not about the destruction of living unborn children, you should instead support the federally funded community health centers located throughout this country. These outnumber Planned Parenthood centers twenty to one and actually focus on health care. Planned Parenthood's core mission, *by its own admission*, is *not* health care. Its core mission is abortion—pure and simple. That's Planned Parenthood.

· Alcorn, *ProLife Answers*, 146–50.

- "Fact Sheet: Reallocating Planned Parenthood's Federal Funding to Comprehensive Health Centers," Charlotte Lozier Institute, March 7, 2017, https://lozierinstitute. org/fact-sheet-reallocating-planned-parenthoods-federal-funding-to-comprehensive-health-centers/.
- Alexandra Desanctis, "Planned Parenthood's President Admits Abortion Is Group's 'Core Mission,'" National Review, January 8, 2019, https://www.nationalreview. com/corner/planned-parenthoods-president-admits-abortion-is-groups-core-mission/.

SECOND REBUTTAL

And here's further proof that abortion, not health care, is Planned Parenthood's core mission: In 2020, Planned Parenthood forfeited sixty million dollars in federal funding—money that could have been used to truly help women—simply because it would have interfered with their abortion industry. Planned Parenthood's core mission is the abortion of unborn children—pure and simple.

- Helen Luan, "Planned Parenthood Leaves Title X, Forfeits $60 Million Annually in Federal Funds," The BL, August 21, 2019, https://thebl.com/us-news/ planned-parenthood-leaves-title-x-forfeits-60-million-annually-in-federal-funds.html.

THIRD REBUTTAL

Look. Does Planned Parenthood provide some important health care services in addition to their barbaric abortion practices? Of course they do. But I simply cannot be supportive of the PAP smear going on in

Room One, while a baby is being dismembered in Room Two. It's that simple.

FOURTH REBUTTAL

Let me tell you three facts that sum up what Planned Parenthood is all about:

- They are the most prolific killer of unborn children in the country (a third of a million babies each year).

- Particularly the children of blacks and minorities; and

- They then sell their body parts for profit.

That's Planned Parenthood.

U.S.

After Fending Off Pandemic Challenger, Planned Parenthood Retains Title For Most Americans Killed In 2020

November 24th, 2020 · Babylonbee.com

U.S.—After fending off a deadly pandemic that killed hundreds of thousands of people, Planned Parenthood proudly announced that they will still earn the title for most Americans killed in a given year.

Pro-Choice Argument
#62

ABORTION IS ONLY A TINY FRACTION (3%) OF THE IMPORTANT HEALTH-CARE SERVICES PROVIDED BY PLANNED PARENTHOOD.

REBUTTAL

That "3%" number has been proven to be a complete fabrication—an accounting deception. For example, when a woman undergoes a second-trimester abortion at Planned Parenthood—*dilatation of her cervix, dismemberment of her baby, vacuuming out the baby's broken body, scraping her uterus, disposing the baby's body, and then cleaning up the gory mess*—Planned Parenthood claims this extremely invasive surgical procedure somehow accounts for only about 20% of the services provided to her that day; her "counseling and related services" constitute the other 80%. Clearly, such accounting is a sham.

- Alexandra Desanctis, "What Planned Parenthood's Annual Report Proves," National Review, January 4, 2018, https://www.nationalreview.com/2018/01/planned-parenthoods-annual-report-disproves-its-own-lies.

- "PragerU Exposes Planned Parenthood Deception," PragerU, February 19, 2018, https://www.prageru.com/press-release/prageru-exposes-planned-parenthood-deception.

- Abby Johnson, "Exposing the Planned Parenthood Business Model," The Hill, April 4, 2011, https://thehill. com/blogs/congress-blog/politics/153699-exposing-the-planned-parenthood-business-model.

"Pro-Life is the simple idea that all life is precious."   —LILA ROSE

"A child is not a choice."   —ANONYMOUS

PRO-CHOICE ARGUMENT #63

FIRE-AT-THE-FERTILITY-CLINIC HYPOTHETICAL:
"A RAGING FIRE SURGES THROUGH A FERTILITY CLINIC.
YOU HAPPEN TO BE WALKING BY AND CAN SAVE EITHER
A FIVE-YEAR-OLD CHILD CAUGHT IN THE INFERNO, OR A
CANISTER MARKED '1,000 LIVING EMBRYOS.'
WHICH DO YOU SAVE?"

[Abortion advocates believe this is their "gotcha" moment—that if you choose to save the five-year-old child instead of the 1,000 living embryos, you are admitting that those embryos have no intrinsic value and/or are not "living beings." *Gotcha!*]

FIRST REBUTTAL

Pro-Life advocates prioritize the life of the "born" over the "unborn." This is why abortion bans will always include a legal exception for cases where the life of the mother is at risk.

- Alcorn, *ProLife Answers*, 222.

SECOND REBUTTAL

Choosing to prioritize one life over another does not negate the sanctity of the other life. For example, what if, instead, there were two young children in the fire, and you could save only one. Does that mean the one you did not save had no intrinsic value, was not a person, or was not alive? Of course not.

It simply means you made your best assessment and prioritized one life over another. Perhaps you contemplated the following:

- Which life would feel pain if burned in a fire?
- Which is more likely to live a full life? (Most embryos in fertility clinics will be callously discarded.)
- The sadness of losing a five-year-old would be more severe than losing an embryo, based on attachments, emotion, and the like.

THIRD REBUTTAL

The hypothetical is meaningless because intentional killing (abortion) and accidental death (the inability to rescue someone from a fire) are different moral issues entirely.

- Ben Shapiro, "The Best Pro-Abortion Argument ever, Debunked," The Ben Shapiro Show, Oct 17, 2017, YouTube video, 2:45, https://www.youtube.com/watch?v=zMyEu3hSjX0.

Pro-Choice Argument #64

> I DON'T CARE IF IT'S ALIVE OR IF IT'S HUMAN AND A PERSON. WHILE IT LIVES IN MY BODY, I CAN KILL IT IF I WANT TO.

FIRST REBUTTAL

Well, no one's going to accuse you of mincing words, and I respect your candor, though perhaps not your compassion. I just can't agree that it's OK to kill a living human baby—outside or inside the uterus—for the convenience of the mother.

SECOND REBUTTAL

I understand your position, but may I ask you a question: If you believe a woman should be fully free to abort her baby, how do you feel about the following:

- Sex-selective abortions: "I'm aborting this baby because it's a girl. I only want sons."
- Gay-gene selective abortions: "I would never want a gay son."
- Race-selective abortions: "I would never want a black baby."

Do any of these scenarios disturb you at all? If so, why?

PRO-CHOICE ARGUMENT #65

[ANY CONFUSED, VAGUE, OR DISINGENUOUS ARGUMENT ABOUT "BEING ALIVE" OR "PERSONHOOD" OR "SENTIENCE" OR "WOMEN'S HEALTH CARE" OR . . . THAT IS CLEARLY JUST AN EXCUSE TO COVER FOR THE DEMAND FOR "SEX WITHOUT CONSEQUENCES."]

REBUTTAL

Why don't we just cut to the chase. The truth is that your arguments about whether a fetus is "alive" or "human" or a "person" or "viable" or "sentient" or "deserving of rights," or your debates about "science" or "misogyny," are not actually your concern. In fact, all your arguments really boil down to one proposition: *sex should be without consequences.* And you are willing to do anything—even kill the unborn—to preserve that goal. I just don't believe that being a burden on someone is justification for you killing them.

· Shapiro, "March for Life Speech."
· Alcorn, "Does a Fetus in the First Trimester Have Value?"

Pro-Choice Argument #66

[ANY AD HOMINEM ATTACK OF YOUR CHOICE
(ATTACKING THE PERSON, NOT THEIR ARGUMENT):
"YOU'RE JUST A MISOGYNIST";
"YOU'RE JUST CALLOUS AND UNCARING";
"YOU'RE JUST A MORON";
"YOU'RE JUST A WACKO RELIGIOUS EXTREMIST";
OR "YOU'RE JUST INTOLERANT."]

REBUTTAL

I don't find it useful to debate *personal* attacks. If, though, you'd actually like to debate the real issues related to abortion, I'd love to discuss them with you— and I promise not to attack you personally. But if your best defense of abortion is simply to attack me personally, then I suspect you really have no legitimate arguments to make.

- Alcorn, *ProLife Answers*, 47.
- Horn, *Persuasive Pro-Life*, 212–16.
- Beckwith, *Politically Correct Death*, 87–90.

VIDEO AND PHOTO LINKS

During discussions and debates about abortion, I am regularly surprised by how little abortion advocates actually know about the developing embryo and fetus. Even more startling, many have absolutely no idea what physically occurs during the act of abortion.

I have found it extremely helpful to have actual *photographs and videos* of the unborn in various stages of development saved on my phone. On many occasions, simply sharing these beautiful images of unborn children has deeply moved abortion advocates.

I also keep *video animations* of the five types of abortion procedures on my phone. On more than one occasion, they have driven fierce proponents of abortion to tears, confessing, "I guess I had no idea what abortion really was. I just didn't know."

These photographs, videos, and animations are often our most powerful tools for conversion.

Keep them on your phone and be ready to use them at a moment's notice.

If you are interested in downloading any of these images, videos, or animations, please visit **www.SpeakingForTheUnborn.org.**

"Fewer women would have abortions
if wombs had windows."

—DR. BERNARD NATHANSON
(FORMER ABORTIONIST)

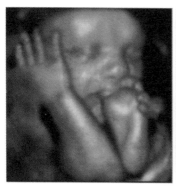 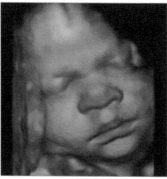

ABORTION AND THE CATHOLIC CHURCH

The *Catechism of the Catholic Church* is an organized presentation of the essential teachings of the Catholic Church with regard to both faith and morals.

On the issue of abortion, the Catechism—in unambiguous language—fully condemns the act of abortion and the act of cooperating with, endorsing, or supporting abortion in any manner:

2270 Human life must be respected and protected absolutely from the moment of conception. From the first moment of his existence, a human being must be recognized as having the rights of a person—among which is the inviolable right of every innocent being to life [cf. CDF, *Donum vitae* I, 1].

Before I formed you in the womb I knew you, and before you were born, I consecrated you. [Jer 1:5; cf. Job 10:8–12; Ps 22:10–11]

My frame was not hidden from you, when I was being made in secret, intricately wrought in the depths of the earth. [Ps 139:15]

2271 Since the first century the Church has affirmed the moral evil of every procured abortion. This teaching has not changed and remains unchangeable. Direct abortion, that is to say, abortion willed either as an end or a means, is gravely contrary to the moral law:

You shall not kill the embryo by abortion and shall not cause the newborn to perish. [*Didache* 2, 2: SCh 248, 148; cf. *Ep. Barnabae* 19, 5: PG 2 777; *Ad Diognetum* 5, 6: PG 2, 1173; Tertullian, *Apol.* 9: PL 1, 319–320]

God, the Lord of life, has entrusted to men the noble mission of safeguarding life, and men must carry it out in a manner worthy of themselves. Life must be protected with the utmost care from the moment of conception: abortion and infanticide are abominable crimes. [GS 51 §3]

2272 Formal cooperation in an abortion constitutes a grave offense. The Church attaches the canonical penalty of excommunication to this crime against human life. "A person who procures a completed abortion incurs excommunication *latae sententiae*" [CIC, can. 1398], "by the very commission of the offense" [CIC, can. 1314], and subject to the conditions provided by Canon Law [cf. CIC, cann. 1323–1324]. The Church does not thereby intend to restrict the scope of mercy. Rather, she makes clear the gravity of the crime committed, the irreparable harm done to the innocent who is put to death, as well as to the parents and the whole of society.

2273 The inalienable right to life of every innocent human individual is a *constitutive element of a civil society and its legislation:*

"The inalienable rights of the person must be recognized and respected by civil society and the political authority. These human rights depend neither on single individuals nor on parents; nor do they represent a concession made by society and the state; they belong to human nature and are inherent in the person by virtue of the creative act from which the person took his origin. Among such fundamental rights one should mention in this regard every human being's right to life and physical integrity from the moment of conception until death" [CDF, *Donum vitae* III].

"The moment a positive law deprives a category of human beings of the protection which civil legislation ought to accord them, the state is denying the equality of all before the law. When the state does not place its power at the service of the rights of each citizen, and in particular of the more vulnerable, the very foundations of a state based on law are undermined. . . . As a consequence of the respect and protection which must be ensured for the unborn child from the moment of conception, the law must provide appropriate penal sanctions for every deliberate violation of the child's rights" [CDF, *Donum vitae* III].

2274 Since it must be treated from conception as a person, the embryo must be defended in its integrity, cared for, and healed, as far as possible, like any other human being.

Prenatal diagnosis is morally licit, "if it respects the life and integrity of the embryo and the human fetus and is directed toward its safe guarding or healing as an individual. . . . It is gravely opposed to the moral law when this is done with the thought of possibly inducing an abortion, depending upon the results: a diagnosis must not be the equivalent of a death sentence" [CDF, Donum vitae I, 2].

2275 "One must hold as licit procedures carried out on the human embryo which respect the life and integrity of the embryo and do not involve disproportionate risks for it, but are directed toward its healing the improvement of its condition of health, or its individual survival" [CDF, Donum vitae I, 3].

"It is immoral to produce human embryos intended for exploitation as disposable biological material" [CDF, Donum vitae I, 5].

"Certain attempts to influence chromosomic or genetic inheritance are not therapeutic but are aimed at producing human beings selected according to sex or other predetermined qualities. Such manipulations are contrary to the personal dignity of the human being and his integrity and identity" [CDF, *Donum vitae* I, 6] which are unique and unrepeatable.

"Any country that accepts abortion is not teaching its people to love, but to use violence to get what they want."

—St. Mother Teresa

Resources for Pregnant Women

Those of us in the Pro-Life movement must always remind ourselves that we cannot limit our efforts to only the banning of abortion. We must also be strong advocates for all mothers—because "abortion is not a sign that women are free, but a sign that they are desperate."[12]

We must work diligently to provide real options and opportunities for these desperate women. We need to make sure that all pregnant mothers understand that the Pro-Life movement is on their side.

Become familiar with the resources available to these women in your area. Make contacts and carry the phone numbers of people and organizations who are ready to offer help.

The following is a list of free and confidential resources for pregnant mothers in need and includes information on a variety of topics:

- Pregnancy counseling
- Emotional support
- Medical care for mother and baby

12   Mathewes-Green, "Abortion: Women's Rights and Wrongs."

- Financial and housing support
- Adoption options (if so desired)
- Domestic violence resources

Let's make sure these frightened women know about these resources!

PREGNANCY HELP, RESOURCES, AND ABORTION ALTERNATIVES

National Life Center Pregnancy Hotline
800-848-5683
www.nationallifecenter.com

Optionline
800-712-4357
www.optionline.org

Bethany Christian Services
800-238-4269
www.bethany.org

Stand Up Girl
www.standupgirl.com/girl-help/need-help-now/

Birthright
800-550-4900
www.birthright.org

Good Counsel Homes
800-723-8331
goodcounselhomes.org

Nightlight Christian Adoptions
502-423-5780
www.nightlight.org

Adoption Network Law Center
800-367-2367
www.adoptionnetwork.com

Safe Haven for Newborns
A confidential safety net for pregnant women or mothers with newborns who do not feel capable of caring for their child and need immediate help.
844-767-2229
www.asafehavenfornewborns.com

Abortion Pill Reversal
For pregnant women who have taken the first dose of the "Abortion Pill" (RU-486) but have not yet taken the second medication (Misoprostol), which is administered twenty-four to forty-eight hours after taking RU-486. This website provides information on medications with the potential to reverse this "medical" abortion process.
877-558-0333
www.abortionpillreversal.com

POST-ABORTION COUNSELING

Hope after Abortion
888-456-4673
www.hopeafterabortion.org

National Domestic Violence Hotline

800-799-7233

Suicide Prevention Hotline

800-273-8255

LEARN ABOUT YOUR GROWING BABY

Pregnant and Panicked? Here's What to Expect during Your Pregnancy

www.whattoexpect.com

Keeping Mom and Baby Healthy during Pregnancy

www.tommys.org/pregnancy-information/
im-pregnant/early-pregnancy/5-things-do-when-you-
find-out-youre-pregnant

Fetal Development: Month by Month (Images and Information)

www.onhealth.com/content/1/
fetal_development_stages

Fetal Development: Week by Week (Images and Information)

www.babycenter.com/fetal-development-week-by-week

Baby Developmental Facts

www.prolifeacrossamerica.org/learn/

Video: "Nine Months in the Womb"
(Fetal Development)
www.youtube.com/watch?v=WH9ZJu4wRUE

Video: "Life in the Womb (9 Months in 4 Minutes)"
(Fetal Development)
www.youtube.com/watch?v=K7kaw40pPYw

Indexed List of Pro-Choice Arguments

Selected Bibliography

Alcorn, Randy. "Does a Fetus in the First Trimester Have Value? Ben Shapiro's Answer to a Pro-Choice College Student." Eternal Perspective Ministries (blog). September 27, 2017. https:// www.epm.org/blog/2017/Sep/27/ fetus-value-ben-shapiro.

———. "Is Abortion Really a Women's Rights Issue?" Chap. 8 in Why Pro-Life? Caring for the Unborn and Their Mothers. Peabody, MA: Hendrickson, 2012.

———. "Is the Unborn Part of the Mother's Body?" Eternal Perspective Ministries. March 29, 2010. https://www.epm.org/resources/2010/Mar/29/ unborn-part-mothers-body/.

———. ProLife Answers to ProChoice Arguments. 3rd ed. Colorado Springs: Multnomah, 2000.

American Adoptions. "How Many Couples Are Waiting to Adopt a Baby?" Accessed August 14, 2021. https://www.americanadoptions.com/pregnant/ waiting_adoptive_families.

American College of Pediatricians. "When Human Life Begins." March 2017. https://acpeds.org/position-statements/ when-human-life-begins.

American Heritage Medical Dictionary, The. Reprint, Boston: Houghton Mifflin, 2008.

Beckwith, Francis J. Politically Correct Death: Answering the Arguments for Abortion Rights. Ada, MI: Baker Books, 1993.

———. Taking Rites Seriously: Law, Politics, and the Reasonableness of Faith. New York: Cambridge University Press, 2015.

Birth Control Federation of America (Planned Parenthood). *Plan Your Family for Health and Happiness.* Copy available in the Sophia Smith Collection at Smith College in Northampton, MA. Accessed August 14, 2021. https://libex.smith.edu/omeka/items/show/440.

Bomberger, Ryan. "No, Abortion Is Not Health Care. It's #FakeHealth." Life Site News. August 1, 2018. https://www.lifesitenews.com/opinion/no-abortion-is-not-health-care.-its-fakehealth.

———. "'Reverend' Rob Schenck's Pro-Abortion Pitch is Pathetic." Townhall. June 8, 2019. https://townhall.com/columnists/ryanbomberger/2019/06/08/reverend-rob-schencks-pro-abortion-pitch-is-pathetic-n2547379.

Camp, Frank. "Watch: Professor Rebuts Three Pro-Abortion Arguments, Notes A 'Profound Difference Between' What Is 'Legal' And What Is 'Moral.' The Daily Wire. March 3, 2019. https://www.dailywire.com/news/watch-professor-rebuts-three-abortion-arguments-frank-camp.

Catholic News Agency. "Poll Finds Two-Thirds of New Yorkers Oppose Late-Term Abortion." March 29, 2019. https://www.catholicnewsagency.com/news/40909/poll-finds-two-thirds-of-new-yorkers-oppose-late-term-abortion.

Charlotte Lozier Institute. "Fact Sheet: Reallocating Planned Parenthood's Federal Funding to Comprehensive Health Centers." March 7, 2017. https://lozierinstitute.org/fact-sheet-reallocating-planned-parenthoods-federal-funding-to-comprehensive-health-centers/.

Cinquanta, Leanna. "Pro-Life Is Not Anti-Women's Rights... Just Anti-Murder." Leanna Cinquanta (blog). February 4, 2017. https://leannacinquanta.com/pro-life-is-not-anti-womens-rights-just-anti-murder/.

Corsini, Dominic. "8 Characteristics of Life in Biology."
Study.com. Accessed October 11, 2021. https://study.
com/academy/lesson/8-characteristics-of-life-in-
biology.html.

Crowder, Steven. "I'm Pro-Life. Change My Mind." November
7, 2017. YouTube video, 1:07:02. https://www.youtube.
com/watch?v=OCSZYJywQPM.

DeLong, Taryn Oesch. "Inside Look: Women Leading the
Pro-Life Movement." April 20, 2020. https://www.
femcatholic.com/post/ facing-goliath-the-women-
leading-the-pro-life-movement.

Desanctis, Alexandra. "Biden and Harris Celebrate *Roe* without
Saying 'Abortion.'" National Review. January 22, 2021.
https://www.nationalreview.com/corner/biden-and-
harris-celebrate-roe-without-saying-abortion/.

———. "Planned Parenthood's President Admits Abortion Is
Group's 'Core Mission.'" National Review. January
8, 2019. https://www.nationalreview.com/corner/
planned-parenthoods-president-admits-abortion-is-
groups-core-mission/.

———. "What Planned Parenthood's Annual Report Proves."
National Review. January 4, 2018. https://www.
nationalreview.com/2018/01/planned-parenthoods-
annual-report-disproves-its-own-lies.

Doctors on Fetal Pain. "Fetal Pain: The Evidence." Updated
February 2013. http://www.doctorsonfetalpain.com.

Doe v. Bolton, 410 U.S. 179 (1972). www.loc.gov/item/
usrep410179/.

Fiano-Chesser, Cassy. "Watch: Abortion Is Never Medically
Necessary, and It's Not Health Care." Live Action News.
December 22, 2018. https://www.liveaction.org/news/
abortion-never-medically-health-care/.

Finer, Lawrence B., Lori F. Frohwirth, Lindsay A Dauphinee, Susheela Singh, and Ann M. Moore. "Reasons US Women Have Abortions: Quantitative and Qualitative Perspectives." *Perspectives on Sexual and Reproductive Health* 37, no. 5 (2005): 110–18.

Fisher, Brian. "Here's How to Stop Any Pro-Choice Argument in Its Tracks." Human Coalition. May 27, 2014. https://www.humancoalition.org/2014/05/27/huco-helps-unravel-thorny-pro-abortion-arguments/.

Foley, Avery. "Is Morality Determined by Its Popularity?" Answers In Genesis. October 13, 2017. https://answersingenesis.org/morality/is-morality-determined-by-its-popularity/.

French, David. "No, Georgia's Heartbeat Bill Won't Imprison Women Who Have Abortions." National Review. May 11, 2019. https://www.nationalreview.com/corner/georgia-heartbeat-bill-will-not-imprison-women-who-have-abortions/.

Gilder, George. *Men and Marriage.* 5th ed. Gretna, LA: Pelican, 2008.

Goldberg, Arthur. "Abortion's Devastating Impact Upon Black Americans." Public Discourse. February 11, 2019. https://www.thepublicdiscourse.com/2019/02/48594/.

Grabianowski, Ed. "10 Overturned Supreme Court Cases." How Stuff Works. November 10, 2010. https://money.howstuffworks.com/10-overturned-supreme-court-cases.htm.

Horn, Trent. *Persuasive Pro-Life: How to Talk about Our Culture's Toughest Issue.* El Cajon, CA: Catholic Answers, 2014.

Jackson, Timothy M. "Why Elective Abortion Can Never Constitute Health Care." The Federalist. January 3, 2018. https://thefederalist.com/2018/01/03/elective-abortion-is-not-healthcare-end-of-story/.

Jacobs, Steve. "I Asked Thousands of Biologists When Life Begins. The Answer Wasn't Popular." Quillette. October 16, 2019. https://quillette.com/2019/10/16/i-asked-thousands-of-biologists-when-life-begins-the-answer-wasnt-popular/.

Johnson, Abby. "Exposing the Planned Parenthood Business Model." The Hill. April 4, 2011. https://thehill.com/blogs/congress-blog/politics/153699-exposing-the-planned-parenthood-business-model.

Kaczor, Christopher. The Ethics of Abortion: Women's Rights, Human Life, and the Question of Justice. 2nd ed. Abingdon, UK: Routledge, 2015.

Kemper, Bryan. Social Justice Begins in the Womb. Magnolia, TX: Lucid Books, 2009.

King, Martin Luther, Jr. "Speaks from the Pulpit on Courage." Transcript of speech delivered at Selma, AL, March 8, 1965. Accessed October 11, 2021. http://faculty.etsu.edu/history/documents/mlkselma.htm.

Klusendorf, Scott. "Stepping up to Defend Life." Focus on the Family, February 25, 2019. YouTube video, 27:53. https://www.youtube.com/watch?v=mzJBrkii0_Y.

Koukl, Greg. "Only One Question." Stand to Reason. February 28, 2013. https://www.str.org/articles/only-one-question#.XPpbIi2ZOg8.

———. "Trotting Out the Toddler." Stand to Reason. May 29, 2013. https://www.str.org/videos/trotting-out-the-toddler.

Kristof, Nicholas. "Bleeding Heart Tightwads." The New York Times. December 20, 2008. https://www.nytimes.com/2008/12/21/opinion/21kristof.html.

Leeman, Jonathan, and Matthew Arbo. "Why Abortion Makes Sense." The Gospel Coalition. June 1, 2016. https://www.thegospelcoalition.org/article/why-abortion-makes-sense/.

Live Action News. "Ben Shapiro Destroys Argument that
a 'Fetus' Isn't a Human Life." Save the Storks.
September 18, 2017. https://savethestorks.com/2017/09/
ben-shapiro-destroys-argument-fetus-isnt-human-life/.

Luan, Helen. "Planned Parenthood Leaves Title X, Forfeits
$60 Million Annually in Federal Funds." The
BL. August 21, 2019. https://thebl.com/us-news/
planned-parenthood-leaves-title-x-forfeits-60-million-
annually-in-federal-funds.html.

Lucky, Ethan, and Skyler Lee. "'No Uterus, No Opinion?'
Why Men Must Speak Out Against Abortion."
Human Defense Initiative. May 29, 2018. https://
humandefense.com/no-uterus-no-opinion/.

Marist Poll and Knights of Columbus. "Americans' Opinions
on Abortion." Life News. January 2019. https://
lifenews-wpengine.netdna-ssl.com/wp-content/
uploads/2019/01/2019MartistAbortionPoll.pdf.

Maternal Mortality in 2005: Estimates Developed by WHO, UNICEF,
UNFPA, and The World Bank. Geneva, CH: World Health
Organization, 2007. http://www.who.int/whosis/
mme_2005.pdf.

Mathewes-Green, Frederica. "Abortion: Women's Rights and
Wrongs." Frederica.com (blog). January 1, 2000. http://
frederica.com/writings/abortion-womens-rights-and-
wrongs.html.

McGuire, Ashley E. "Pro-Life Movement Has Always Been
Driven by Women." The Hill. January 21, 2016. https://
thehill. com/blogs/congress-blog/civil-rights/266470-
pro-life-movement-has-always-been-driven-by-women.

Moore, Keith L., T. V. N. Persaud, and Mark G. Torchia. The
Developing Human: Clinically Oriented Embryology. 10th ed.
Philadelphia: Saunders, 2016.

Moore, Russell. "Trump Reverses Obama's Anti-Religious
    Decree." *The Wall Street Journal.* November 3, 2019.
    https://www.wsj.com/articles/trump-reverses-obamas-
    anti-christian-decree-11572813718.

Mosher, Steven W. "The Repackaging of Margaret Sanger," *The
    Wall Street Journal.* May 5, 1997. https://www.wsj.com/
    articles/SB862769009690799000

New, Michael J. "Abortion Promises Unfulfilled." Public
    Discourse. January 23, 2013. https://www.
    thepublicdiscourse.com/2013/01/7630/.

Odum, Patrick D. "A Child of God: Who Are You?" Heart
    Light. August 8, 2004. https://www.heartlight.org/
    articles/200408/20040808_childofgod.html.

Payne, Daniel, "Here's a Primer on Pro-Life Responses to
    Common Counter-Arguments." The Federalist.
    January 30, 2017. https://thefederalist.com/2017/01/30/
    heres-primer-pro-life-responses-common-counter-
    arguments/.

Ponnuru, Ramesh. *The Party of Death: The Democrats, the Media, the
    Courts, and the Disregard for Human Life.* Washington, DC:
    Regnery, 2006.

PragerU. "PragerU Exposes Planned Parenthood
    Deception." February 19, 2018. https://
    www.prageru.com/press-release/
    prageru-exposes-planned-parenthood-deception.

Prestigiacomo, Amanda. "Watch: Students for Life President
    Demolishes Common Pro-Abortion Talking Point from
    Feminist." The Daily Wire. May 29, 2019. https://www.
    dailywire.com/news/watch-students-life-president-
    demolishes-common-amanda-prestigiacomo.

Rajasekar, Akhil. "Why It Doesn't Matter If the Unborn
Aren't Persons." The Federalist. January 10,
2019. https://thefederalist.com/2019/01/10/
doesnt-matter-unborn-arent-persons/.

Rasmussen Reports. "44% of Pro-Choice Voters Oppose NY
Abortion Law in Their State." February 7, 2019. http://
www.rasmussenreports.com/public_content/politics/
current_events/abortion/44_of_pro_choice_voters_
oppose_ny_abortion_law_in_their_state.

Robinson, Michael. "No Uterus, No Opinion? Should Men Have
a Voice on Abortion?" LifeNews.com. March 1, 2019.
https://www.lifenews.com/2019/03/01/no-uterus-no-
opinion-should-men-have-a-voice-on-abortion/.

Rose, Lila. "On Mars, a single cell would be considered LIFE."
Facebook, December 7, 2018. https://www.facebook.
com/lilagracerose/photos/on-mars-a-single-cell-
would-be-considered-life-however-on-earth-a-human-
being-in/10157034074073000/.

———. "Women don't need to kill their children to pursue
the dreams, goals, and careers that they
want." Facebook, September 5, 2018. https://
www.facebook.com/lilagracerose/posts/
women-dont-need-to-kill-their-children-to-pursue-the-
dreams-goals-and-careers-th/10156802063183000/.

Saad, Lydia. "Americans Divided Over Abortion Debate:
Similar Percentages Call Themselves Pro-Choice and
Pro-Life." Gallup. May 18, 1999. https://news.gallup.
com/poll/3847/americans-divided-over-abortion-
debate.aspx.

Saletan, William. "Do Pro-Lifers Oppose Birth Control?"
Slate. January 15, 2014. https://slate.com/
news-and-politics/2014/01/do-pro-lifers-oppose-birth-
control-polls-say-no.html.

Sanger, Margaret. *The Pivot of Civilization*. New York: Brentano's, 1922.

———. *Woman and the New Race*. New York: Eugenics Publishing Company, 1920.

Schoenwolf, Gary C., Steven Bleyl, Philip Brauer, and Philippa Francis-West. *Larsen's Human Embryology*. 5th ed. Philadelphia: Churchill Livingstone, 2015.

Shapiro, Ben. "Ben Shapiro on Abortion: Evil Is Still Evil Regardless of Identity Politics." January 25, 2018. YouTube video, 2:19. https://www.youtube.com/watch?v=047DSK2mTeo&frags=pl%2Cwn.

———. "Ben Shapiro Shreds Pro-Choice Argument 2019." People Choice, February 13, 2019. YouTube video, 17:31. https://www.youtube.com/watch?v=KQ7h0-kq-kU&frags=pl%2Cwn.=.

———. "Ben Shapiro Torches Arrogant Leftist in Epic Battle over Abortion." Young America's Foundation, July 7, 2018. YouTube video, 2:19. https://www.youtube.com/watch?v=BIQRI0LbGqg&frags=pl%2Cwn.

———. "Can They Feel Pain?" Facebook video. January 22, 2019. https://www.facebook.com/watch/?v=226062301634625.

———. "How Feminism Ruined Marriage." The Daily Wire, October 5, 2018. YouTube video, 4:45. https:// www.youtube.com/watch?v=ILUkWyGfuJA&frags=pl%2Cwn.

———. "March for Life Speech." Presented in Washington, DC, January 17, 2019. https://www.youtube.com/watch?v=NZujFL6OKU4.

———. "Marriage Was Set-Up to Protect Women Because Men are Pigs." YouTube video. September 17, 2019, https://twitter.com/yaf/status/1173952244435304448?lang=en.

Shettles, Landrum Brewer, and David M. Rorvik. *Rites of Life: The Scientific Evidence for Life before Birth*. Grand Rapids: Zondervan, 1983.

Sivak, David. "Fact Check: Have There Been 60 Million Abortions Since Roe v. Wade?" Check Your Fact. July 3, 2018. https://checkyourfact. com/2018/07/03/ fact-check-60-million-abortions/.

Snead, Carter. "A Bioethical Argument against Abortion." EWTN Pro-Life Weekly. March 18, 2017. YouTube video, 3:42. https://www.youtube.com/ watch?v=hbM0hHkwJq0.

Sowell, Thomas. "Who Really Cares?" National Review. November 28, 2006. https://www.nationalreview. com/2006/11/who-really-cares-thomas-sowell/.

Stagnaro, Angelo. "22 Ways to Respond to Common Abortion Questions." Catholic Education Resource Center. 2019. https://www.catholiceducation.org/en/controversy/ abortion/22-ways-to-respond-to-common-abortion-questions.html.

Stark, Paul. "'I'm Personally Pro-Life But' Really Just Means You're Pro-Abortion." LifeNews.com. August 23, 2018. https://www.lifenews.com/2018/08/23/im-personally-pro-life-but-really-just-means-youre-pro-abortion/.

Students for Life of America. "Contraception." Accessed August 16, 2021. https://studentsforlife.org/contraception/.

Szoch, Mary, ed. *The Best Pro-Life Arguments for Secular Audiences*. Washington, DC: Family Research Council, 2021. https://www.frc.org/brochure/ the-best-pro-life-arguments-for-secular-audiences.

VerBruggen, Robert. "Trends in Unmarried Childbearing Point to a Coming Apart." Institute for Family Studies. February 20, 2018. https://ifstudies.org/blog/trends-in-unmarried-childbearing-point-to-a-coming-apart.

Wagner, Stephen. "What Is It?" Life Media Resources. Vimeo video. 2009. https://vimeo.com/3285507.

Walsh, Matt. "Why Sexist Deadbeat Men Love Abortion." The Daily Wire. April 24, 2019. https://www.dailywire.com/news/46379/walsh-why-sexist-deadbeat-men-love-abortion-matt-walsh.

Watts, Jay. "Acorns and Embryos." Merely Human Ministries. August 28, 2019. https://merelyhumanministries.org/acorns-and-embryos/.

Photo Credits

Page 5: Nilsson.

Page 7: Shutterstock.

Page 15: Shutterstock.

Page 21: Dr. Steven O'Connor. Used with permission.

Page 25: Dr. Steven A. Christie.

Page 26: Babylon Bee. "'A Fetus Is Just a Clump of Cells,' Says Slightly Older, Larger Clump of Cells." June 4, 2021. https://babylonbee.com/news/a-fetus-is-just-a-clump-of-cells-says-slightly-older-larger-clump-of-cells. Used with permission.

Page 29: Babylon Bee. "Joyful Pro-Choice Mother Throws Fetus Shower." December 23, 2016. https://babylonbee.com/news/joyful-pro-choice-mother-throws-fetus-shower. Used with permission.

Page 32: Babylon Bee. "Democrats Offer Compromise That Unborn Babies Are Three-Fifths of a Person." February 28, 2021. https://babylonbee.com/news/democrats-offer-compromise-that-unborn-babies-are-35-of-a-person. Used with permission.

Page 45: Nilsson.

Page 46: Shutterstock; Dr. Steven A. Christie.

Page 47: Babylon Bee. "Ultrasound Shows Unborn Baby Holding 'Keep Your Laws Off My Body' Sign." March 16, 2018. https://babylonbee.com/news/ultrasound-shows-unborn-baby-holding-keep-your-laws-off-my-body-sign. Used with permission.

Page 53: Flickr.

Page 61: Nilsson.

Page 64: Babylon Bee. "Democrats: 'Without Abortion, Women Might Have To Settle for Having 7 Kids and Sitting on the Highest Court in the Land.'" September 26, 2020. https://babylonbee.com/news/democrats-without-abortion-women-might-have-to-settle-for-having-7-kids-and-sitting-on-the-highest-court-in-the-land. Used with permission.

Page 65: Nilsson.

Page 81: Nilsson.

Page 87: Nilsson.

Page 91: Babylon Bee. "Close One: This Baby Was Almost Born into Poverty but His Mother Killed Him in the Nick of Time." May 16, 2019. https://babylonbee.com/news/close-one-this-baby-was-almost-born-into-poverty-but-his-mother-killed-him-in-the-nick-of-time. Used with permission.

Page 98: Babylon Bee. "Planned Parenthood Distances Themselves from Margaret Sanger by Continuing Her Legacy." April 24, 2021. https://babylonbee.com/news/planned-parenthood-distances-themselves-from-margaret-sanger-by-continuing-her-legacy.

Page 101: Shutterstock.

Page 113: Babylon Bee. "After Fending Off Pandemic Challenger, Planned Parenthood Retains Title for Most Americans Killed in 2020." November 24, 2020. https://babylonbee.com/news/after-fending-off-pandemic-challenger-planned-parenthood-retains-title-for-most-americans-killed-in-2020. Used with permission.

Page 121: Shutterstock.

Page 123: Public domain.

ABOUT THE AUTHOR

Dr. Steven Christie is a physician, specializing in onco-logic radiology and body imaging. He is a Diplomate of the American Board of Radiology. He is also an attorney and member of the Florida Bar.

Aside from his medical and legal work, Dr. Christie also lectures regularly on today's pressing social issues, particularly marriage, family, and the dignity of life.

Dr. Christie is the author of PET/CT MD, an interactive medical textbook for oncologic radiologists (projected publication date: March 2022).

He and his wife, Dr. Grazie Christie, live in the Miami area and are the proud parents of five children.